To Be a Disciple

OTHER TITLES BY BRUCE TAYLOR

The Word in the Wind

No Business as Usual

Looking Up at Love

Life Woven into God

Between Advents

Christ's New Address

Love Walks on Wounded Feet

God at Work

What Happens Next?

Truth Be Told

Practicing the Promise

To Be a Disciple

More Sermons for the Lectionary, Year C,
Pentecost through Christ the King

BRUCE L. TAYLOR

WIPF & STOCK · Eugene, Oregon

TO BE A DISCIPLE
More Sermons for the Lectionary, Year C, Pentecost through Christ the King

Copyright © 2024 Bruce L. Taylor. All rights reserved. Except for brief quotations in critical publications or reviews, no part of this book may be reproduced in any manner without prior written permission from the publisher. Write: Permissions, Wipf and Stock Publishers, 199 W. 8th Ave., Suite 3, Eugene, OR 97401.

Wipf & Stock
An Imprint of Wipf and Stock Publishers
199 W. 8th Ave., Suite 3
Eugene, OR 97401

www.wipfandstock.com

PAPERBACK ISBN: 979-8-3852-2672-6
HARDCOVER ISBN: 979-8-3852-2673-3
EBOOK ISBN: 979-8-3852-2674-0

102224

Unless otherwise noted, scripture quotations are from Common Bible: New Revised Standard Version Bible, copyright © 1989 National Council of the Churches of Christ in the United States of America. Used by permission. All rights reserved worldwide. Emphasis added.

Scripture quotations marked (RSV) are from Revised Standard Version of the Bible, copyright © 1946, 1952, and 1971 National Council of the Churches of Christ in the United States of America. Used by permission. All rights reserved.

Excerpts from *No Great Mischief* by Alistair MacLeod, copyright (C) 1999 by Alistair MacLeod. Used by permission of W. W. Norton & Company, Inc. All rights reserved.

In memory of
Oscar and Mary Wall

Contents

Introduction   xi

THE DAY OF PENTECOST
First Presbyterian Church, Dodge City, Kansas—June 4, 1995
Acts 2:1–21, Romans 8:14–17, John 14:8–17, 25–27
"The Birthday Gift"   1

TRINITY SUNDAY
Spanish Springs Presbyterian Church, Sparks, Nevada—June 3, 2007
Proverbs 8:1–4, 22–31, Romans 5:1–5, John 16:12–15
"Living in a Mystery"   4

NINTH SUNDAY IN ORDINARY TIME
1 Kings 18:20–39, Galatians 1:1–12, Luke 7:1–10
"Who Is Your God?"   9

TENTH SUNDAY IN ORDINARY TIME
Spanish Springs Presbyterian Church, Sparks, Nevada—June 6, 2010
1 Kings 17:8–24, Galatians 1:11–24, Luke 7:11–17
"Crossing Boundaries"   14

ELEVENTH SUNDAY IN ORDINARY TIME
Spanish Springs Presbyterian Church, Sparks, Nevada—June 10, 2007
1 Kings 21:1–21a, Galatians 2:15–21, Luke 7:36—8:3
"Holier Than Jesus?"   20

TWELFTH SUNDAY IN ORDINARY TIME
Spanish Springs Presbyterian Church, Sparks, Nevada—June 20, 2010
1 Kings 19:1–15a, Galatians 3:23–29, Luke 8:26–39
"God in Real Time"   26

THIRTEENTH SUNDAY IN ORDINARY TIME
Spanish Springs Presbyterian Church, Sparks, Nevada—July 1, 2007
2 Kings 2:1–2, 6–14, Galatians 5:1, 13–25, Luke 9:51–62
"To Be a Disciple"   31

FOURTEENTH SUNDAY IN ORDINARY TIME
First Presbyterian Church, Dodge City, Kansas—June 28, 1998
2 Kings 5:1–14, Galatians 6:1–16, Luke 10:1–11, 16–20
"So Much for Pride"   **36**

FIFTEENTH SUNDAY IN ORDINARY TIME
Amos 7:7–17, Colossians 1:1–14, Luke 10:25–37
"What God Commands"   **41**

SIXTEENTH SUNDAY IN ORDINARY TIME
Spanish Springs Presbyterian Church, Sparks, Nevada—July 18, 2010
Amos 8:1–12, Colossians 1:15–28, Luke 10:38–42
"Upsetting the Basket"   **48**

SEVENTEENTH SUNDAY IN ORDINARY TIME
Spanish Springs Presbyterian Church, Sparks, Nevada—July 29, 2001
Hosea 1:2–10, Colossians 2:6–15, Luke 11:1–13
"The Anguish of God"   **54**

EIGHTEENTH SUNDAY IN ORDINARY TIME
Spanish Springs Presbyterian Church, Sparks, Nevada—August 5, 2001
Hosea 11:1–11, Colossians 3:1–11, Luke 12:13–21
"Focus on a Far Horizon"   **60**

NINETEENTH SUNDAY IN ORDINARY TIME
Spanish Springs Presbyterian Church, Sparks, Nevada—August 12, 2001
Isaiah 1:1, 10–20, Hebrews 11:1–3, 8–16, Luke 12:32–40
"The School of Hope"   **66**

TWENTIETH SUNDAY IN ORDINARY TIME
Spanish Springs Presbyterian Church, Sparks, Nevada—August 19, 2001
Isaiah 5:1–7, Hebrews 11:29—12:2, Luke 12:49–56
"Fire on the Earth"   **72**

TWENTY-FIRST SUNDAY IN ORDINARY TIME
Spanish Springs Presbyterian Church, Sparks, Nevada—August 26, 2001
Jeremiah 1:4–10, Hebrews 12:18–29, Luke 13:10–17
"Heaven on Earth"   **77**

TWENTY-SECOND SUNDAY IN ORDINARY TIME
Spanish Springs Presbyterian Church, Sparks, Nevada—August 29, 2010
Jeremiah 2:4–13, Hebrews 13:1–8, 15–16, Luke 14:1, 7–14
"The Trouble with Angels"   **83**

TWENTY-THIRD SUNDAY IN ORDINARY TIME
First Presbyterian Church, Dodge City, Kansas—September 6, 1998
Jeremiah 18:1–11, Philemon 1–21, Luke 14:25–33
"Pray, and Do the Right Thing" 88

TWENTY-FOURTH SUNDAY IN ORDINARY TIME
Spanish Springs Presbyterian Church, Sparks, Nevada—September 12, 2004
Jeremiah 4:11–12, 22–28, 1 Timothy 1:12–17, Luke 15:1–10
"Dinner Will Be Late" 93

TWENTY-FIFTH SUNDAY IN ORDINARY TIME
Spanish Springs Presbyterian Church, Sparks, Nevada—September 23, 2007
Jeremiah 8:18—9:1, 1 Timothy 2:1–7, Luke 16:1–13
"Isn't He the God of All?" 100

TWENTY-SIXTH SUNDAY IN ORDINARY TIME
Lutheran Church of the Master, Lakewood, Colorado—September 25, 2022
Amos 6:1a, 4–7, 1 Timothy 6:6–19, Luke 16:19–31
"Who's Lying at Our Gate?" 106

TWENTY-SEVENTH SUNDAY IN ORDINARY TIME
Spanish Springs Presbyterian Church, Sparks, Nevada—October 7, 2007
Lamentations 1:1–6, 2 Timothy 1:1–14, Luke 17:5–10
"From Generation to Generation" 111

TWENTY-EIGHTH SUNDAY IN ORDINARY TIME
Spanish Springs Presbyterian Church, Sparks, Nevada—October 10, 2010
Jeremiah 29:1, 4–7, 2 Timothy 2:8–15, Luke 17:11–19
"A Blessing to the Nations" 116

TWENTY-NINTH SUNDAY IN ORDINARY TIME
Spanish Springs Presbyterian Church, Sparks, Nevada—October 21, 2001
Jeremiah 31:27–34, 2 Timothy 3:14—4:5, Luke 18:1–8
"The Other Side of Judgment" 121

THIRTIETH SUNDAY IN ORDINARY TIME
First Presbyterian Church, Dodge City, Kansas—October 29, 1995
Joel 2:23–32, 2 Timothy 4:6–8, 16–18, Luke 18:9–14
"Measuring Up to Heaven" 127

ALL SAINTS' DAY
First Presbyterian Church, Ponca City, Oklahoma—November 1, 2013
Daniel 7:1–3, 15–18, Ephesians 1:11–23, Luke 6:20–31
"No Church, No Body" 132

THIRTY-FIRST SUNDAY IN ORDINARY TIME
Spanish Springs Presbyterian Church, Sparks, Nevada—November 4, 2007
Habakkuk 1:1–4; 2:1–4, 2 Thessalonians 1:1–4, 11–12, Luke 19:1–10
"Touched by God"   137

THIRTY-SECOND SUNDAY IN ORDINARY TIME
Haggai 1:15b—2:9, 2 Thessalonians 2:1–5, 13–17, Luke 20:27–38
"The God of the Living"   142

THIRTY-THIRD SUNDAY IN ORDINARY TIME
First Presbyterian Church, Dodge City, Kansas—November 19, 1995
Isaiah 65:17–25, 2 Thessalonians 3:6–13, Luke 21:5–19
"This Is Good News?"   147

CHRIST THE KING SUNDAY
Spanish Springs Presbyterian Church, Sparks, Nevada—November 21, 2010
Jeremiah 23:1–6, Colossians 1:11–20, Luke 23:33–43
"The Kingdom Is Now"   151

EVENING BEFORE THE NATIONAL DAY OF THANKSGIVING
Spanish Springs Presbyterian Church, Sparks, Nevada—November 24, 2010
Deuteronomy 8:1–10, 1 Timothy 2:1–7, Matthew 6:25–33
"Life as Thanksgiving"   156

Appendix   161

MORNING PRAYER   163
Spanish Springs Presbyterian Church, Sparks, Nevada—September 11, 2002
Job 29:1–6; 30:1–2, 16–31, Acts 14:19–28, John 11:1–16

TWENTIETH SUNDAY IN ORDINARY TIME
Spanish Springs Presbyterian Church, Sparks, Nevada—August 15, 2010
Isaiah 5:1–7, Hebrews 11:29—12:2, Luke 12:49–56
"Keeping Faith"   166

NEVADA INTERFAITH COUNCIL FOR WORKER JUSTICE
Exodus 33:12–23, Romans 13:1–7, Matthew 22:15–22
"The Things That Are God's"   171

List of Sources Cited   177

Introduction

Many years ago, when I was departing one pastorate to begin another, a parishioner from the congregation who had volunteered to help me load the rental truck with our household belongings in preparation for the move paused to comment that he was sorry to see me leave the church. He concluded by saying, "I don't think that I had ever before heard anyone preach about discipleship." I looked at him in disbelief, but he was obviously sincere. I was astounded that this forty-something weekly worshiper, a ruling elder active in every aspect of the church, had spent many years listening to sermons prior to my arrival as pastor without being able to identify a single instance of encouragement in what Matthew says Jesus instructed his apostles was to be their mission.

Perhaps it is indicative of the confusion of pastoral roles that has become evident in the past several decades within an institution desperately claiming the relevancy of its shrinking iceberg adrift in a sea boiling with secularist aspirations, but Sunday morning and other worship occasions in quite a few pulpits seem more about therapy than gospel, more centered on pleasant thoughts than prophetic proclamation. No preacher should labor intentionally to be belligerent and insulting, insensitive to hurts or oblivious to vulnerability. Yet, the Bible, upon which, in historic Reformed understanding, preaching should be founded, is not primarily concerned with developing a positive self-image or even healthy family dynamics. Nor is it, contrary to much preaching in medieval times and still in some quarters today, primarily devoted to convincing people that they are going to hell (or that their neighbors are going to hell). And it is definitely not an occasion for promoting the pastor's personal opinion or private prejudice.

Salvation has to do with faith, and, while no one is in a position to measure the faith of another, the Bible is insistent that we understand, for ourselves, and act upon our understanding, that it is all related to repentance (changing one's pursuit of self-this and -that and turning instead toward the ways of God, shown most perfectly in Jesus' way to the cross) and trusting God completely and loving God with all of one's heart and mind and soul and strength and, therefore, loving one's neighbor as oneself. It has to do with listening to Christ, learning from Christ, dining with and upon Christ, and following Christ, including in the business of caring for others' physical needs, welcoming and befriending and protecting and forgiving and defending and encouraging them in the ways of obedience to God at work through the Holy Spirit. We are commissioned, through the risen Lord's instruction to the remaining eleven original disciples, faithfully to *make* disciples, which means first to *be* disciples. What could be a more relevant task for the church in any age?

All of this points to the significance of preaching and its paramount position in the minister's job description so that it may be vitally important in the life of the worshiper. Faithful preaching, and faithful preparation for preaching, is a sacred trust, with emphasis on both of those words. It is a privilege. It is a commission. It is a task. It has to do with salvation. It has to do with God's purpose for creation. It has to do with Christ's intention for the church. It has to do with the Spirit's access to the heart of the believer and the collective heart of the believing community. Any single word or phrase may be the Spirit's inspiring means of penetrating stubbornness or incomprehension; a steadfast weekly hewing to the truths of the gospel may nurture a lifetime's progressive revelation of heaven's agenda for the business of living. It must not be squandered. It must not be trivialized. It demands the best work of the preacher as it demands the fullest attention of the worshiper. It has the potential of being, has the expectation of being, the word of God for that people in that place at that time. If, on occasion, it fails in any of those things, it must also be the preacher's existential testimony to the forgiveness of God, in which she or he must trust and upon which she or he must rely. It is a yielding to a call, confirmed in ordination and installation through the prayerful affirmation of the church as witnessed in the polity to which the body of believers has given consent and for which the body of believers has asked God's leading and upon which the body of believers has asked God's blessing. As was true of the prophets in scripture, the summons to preach is not a call to popularity or earthly acclaim. It is a call to truth, honesty, and the manifestation of God's will as illumined by scripture, all prompted and made possible by the gift-bestowing Holy Spirit. Care and discipline, prayer and study, should be the routine which knows no higher application of the preacher's time and intellect and devotion, save, as homiletician David Buttrick once observed in a Des Moines Presbytery preaching workshop I attended, the pastoral functions of holding the hands of the dying and comforting the bereaved. Surely, it should not be relegated to the left-over moments following all the other obligations of clerical life, certainly not the proverbial late Saturday night.

This book is the final compilation in a homiletical journey through two cycles of the three-year Common Lectionary of scripture readings for

Sundays and feast days, whose utility and advantages I have addressed in previous volumes. It includes three sermons written specifically for this book and not yet preached to a congregation, and a sampling of story-form sermons as well as three appended sermons prepared for extraordinary occasions. Some were difficult to write, from an exegetical view, while others fairly wrote themselves. Some were difficult to preach because of the bluntness of the scripture upon which they were based or the sober times during which they were originally delivered. Quite a few startled me when I saw where the scriptures had led me. In all, I realized that I had first been preaching to myself, a sinner in need of grace and a believer in need of Christian community, praying for the Spirit's leading and strength in loving as Christ loved, hoping for the congregation's support in the common effort, parishioners and pastor, of discerning God's will and growing together in faithful discipleship.

The Day of Pentecost
First Presbyterian Church, Dodge City, Kansas
June 4, 1995

Acts 2:1–21
Romans 8:14–17
John 14:8–17, 25–27

"The Birthday Gift"

As I was growing up, I remember having several birthday parties, with many friends and family members present, and I also remember attending quite a few birthday parties for classmates and other children that I knew. There usually came a time, at these parties, for opening the gifts that had been brought, and everyone's anticipation would build to that point, when the boxes wrapped up in paper and bows would be opened, and the mystery would be solved of what each one contained. Some of my friends, though, came from homes where gift-opening was a private affair—when we lived in El Paso, Texas, I noticed that it was the custom in many Hispanic families not to unwrap presents in front of others. The reason for that seemed to be to ensure that no one would ever be embarrassed by the relative lavishness or simplicity of the gift. Although that took away some of the fun for the partygoers, it represented a gentle wisdom from which our own competitive and materialistic culture could well benefit. For, at the parties where the gifts were opened in front of everybody, the children naturally compared the expense and pleasure of the gifts in a way which they were not yet old enough to realize showed unkindness and ingratitude.

One of the usual comparisons to be made was between gifts that were toys or amusements, and gifts that were what we used to call "practical"— the difference between a doll or a kite or a paint set and a shirt or socks or sweater. We children who came from relatively affluent families where our basic needs of food and shelter and clothing were met without concern, and in a way that we took very much for granted, usually greeted our presents of clothing with a groan. We felt somehow cheated in our hope that the present that was shaped suspiciously like a department store carton might in fact contain something surprisingly entertaining. Even such useful gifts as dictionaries and rulers did not seem like real birthday presents. What we all hoped for was something that our parents would consider completely frivolous, and we were disappointed when it was something as practical as a coat.

As we grow older, and hopefully less susceptible to the wiles of advertisers and the whims of fad, most of us appreciate more the thoughtfulness that goes into "practical gifts." We tend to be more grateful for the concern that the gift-giver had that we should be warm and dry or have the basic study tools necessary to do well in school or be supplied with articles that we use every day in our workplace at home or shop or office. The gifts that are the most important, after all, are not the ones that simply amuse us, but items that are useful, tools that help us do our best, things that help us to fulfill our potential. But some of us still prefer gifts that are more an extravagance than a necessity, and some of us prize most of all gifts that feed our vanity.

On the Christian calendar, the period from Easter to Pentecost celebrates the beginning of the Christian church; it marks the time when Jesus, raised by God from the dead, appeared to the disciples and taught them how all that had happened had fulfilled the scriptures, and how they were now to minister in his name and help usher in the kingdom. But Jesus could not remain with his disciples indefinitely—perhaps he knew that he must withdraw from them his physical presence if they were ever to have the courage and conviction to preach and teach and heal and forgive and bless as he had done. In John's Gospel, as we read today, Jesus promised even before the crucifixion that the Father would send an Advocate, the Holy Spirit, to teach and remind the disciples, to encourage and prod them in their ministry. In Luke's Gospel, the promise came just before Jesus was raised up into heaven to sit in a place of power and glory. The followers of Jesus could expect to receive a gift—a very special and very important, a very useful and very meaningful gift—the gift of the Holy Spirit, to enable them to be Christ's body present and at work in the world as Christ's own eyes and ears and mouth and hands and feet, extending his ministry of compassion and reconciliation and forgiveness and love beyond Palestine into every corner of the world. And, according to the book of Acts, "when the day of Pentecost had come, they were all together in one place. And suddenly from heaven there came a sound like the rush of a violent wind, and it filled the entire house where they were sitting. Divided tongues, as of fire, appeared among them, and a tongue rested on each of them. All of them were filled with the Holy Spirit" (Acts 2:1–4). And the rest of the book of Acts tells the story of what the Holy Spirit equipped and motivated those people to do.

Jesus had promised, and God had given, just the right gift to the church on its birthday—the powerful, comforting, encouraging, and continuous presence of Christ himself in the Holy Spirit to enable and prompt those who believe in him to do the same sorts of things that he did: to open eyes and ears long closed, to warm hearts and hopes long cold, to arouse compassion and zeal long forgotten, to move hands and feet long idle. Some people have misunderstood the gift, supposing, for instance, that praying in tongues marks a sort of superior Christianity, constitutes a personal reward or a secret requirement for faith. The gift of the Holy Spirit was and still is a *useful* one, not given as an extravagance, not meant to serve our vanity, but to help us meet the real needs of other people through humble acts of service. It was and is given not to separate Christians from the world by elevating us above our fellow men and women, but to unify us for the task of involving ourselves in redeeming the pain and suffering of the world. It was and is for the purpose of transforming believers from the self-centered tendencies of all humankind into disciples of Christ who gave himself up on the cross and poured himself out for the sake of others. It was and is just what the church needs if it is to be faithful in carrying the ministry of Jesus of Nazareth into every corner of the globe—Africa, India, China, Kansas—so that all people, regardless of language, nationality, race, economic condition, or whatever other distinction, may know the love and mercy and hope of God in Jesus Christ.

That is why we celebrate Pentecost, God's out-pouring of the Holy Spirit and the birth of the church. That is why we give thanks to God for being faithful to the church, the very body of Christ, from the very instant that it was born. That is why the Holy Spirit is the very best birthday gift God could give the church.

Trinity Sunday

Spanish Springs Presbyterian Church, Sparks, Nevada

June 3, 2007

Proverbs 8:1–4, 22–31
Romans 5:1–5
John 16:12–15

"Living in a Mystery"

Today is Trinity Sunday. Unlike Easter and Epiphany and Christmas and Ascension Day, *this* annual feast day of the church does not commemorate any particular event in the life of Christ. Unlike Pentecost, it does not commemorate any particular event in the history of the church. It is, instead, a day set aside for celebrating a theological truth. Trinity Sunday originated in Western Europe in the tenth century and spread only slowly until the church at Rome adopted it officially in the fourteenth century. Protestants inherited it from Catholicism, along with the rest of the church year.

The slowness in adopting the *day* as part of the Christian calendar echoes the slowness of the Christian church in articulating the *doctrine* of the Trinity. It comes as a surprise to most people that the word "Trinity" appears nowhere in the Bible. Jesus spoke about God and spoke of himself as the Son and spoke about the Holy Spirit, but he is not remembered as defining the exact relationship between all three. Paul wrote of God and Christ and the Holy Spirit, but none of his letters sets forth a precise explanation of how all three are one and the same God. It was the actual experience of the church that led theologians eventually to express in *human language* the *divine reality* that the Creator and Deliverer and Law-giver witnessed to in the *Old* Testament, and the Redeemer and Healer and Forgiver witnessed to in the *New* Testament, and the powerful and inspiring presence who was at work in hearts and minds and events in *both* testaments, are *one*

God, united in *purpose*, united in *love*, united in the *Godhead*. People who met and listened to and were befriended and healed and fed and forgiven by Jesus *before* the *crucifixion* saw in him the fullness of God. People who met and ate and worshiped together in Christ's name *after* the *resurrection* sensed his presence still among them, and powerfully so. For those very first Christians, there was no need to write creeds or treatises, no need to formulate in precise terms a cogent explanation of the truth that they all had come to know instinctively based on their shared first-hand experience. But gradually, perhaps first in the words spoken as people were baptized, the church recognized that to speak of God meant to speak of the Father, the Son, and the Holy Spirit, and that by speaking about *any* of those three—Father, Son, Holy Spirit—the church was speaking about *God*.

The words that the church adopted to express the Trinity were and remain imperfect. The relationship between the Father, Son, and Holy Spirit, we must admit, is a divine mystery, and any attempt to *describe* a divine mystery can never be complete, can never be exact, can never be adequate. But the articulation of the doctrine represented a maturity of reflection that only time and the work of the Holy Spirit could produce, and the term "Trinity" has become a short-hand expression that communicates a reality lying at the heart of our faith, even though no two of us understand it in precisely the same way, and each of our efforts must always fall short. *This side of heaven, at least, the Trinity is and will always remain a mystery—* literally, something that cannot be explained, something beyond human comprehension.

I think that Jesus was wise, and Paul was too, in not trying to define the Trinity in words. Eventually, of course, circumstances made it necessary for the church to do so; some things that were being taught about Christ, in particular, were jeopardizing the faith and dividing the church. But the Gospels show that Jesus was content to invite his followers to *benefit from* the relationship between the Father, Son, and Holy Spirit, even to be a *part* of it. At one point, he spoke of the Holy Spirit as "the Spirit of truth" (John 16:13) who would glorify him, Jesus. The Spirit did not represent a truth *new* and *different* from what Jesus had been saying and doing; indeed, the Spirit would *reinforce* it, bring it to bear on *new situations, enlarge* it. "All that the Father has is mine" (16:15a), Jesus told the disciples the night before the crucifixion. What greater oneness could there be than that?

But the unity of the Trinity isn't just about the Father, the Son, and the Holy Spirit. "I am in the Father, and you in me, and I in you" (14:20), Jesus declared to his disciples at another point. And "[the Spirit] will take what is mine and declare it to you" (16:14). To be united to Christ is to be admitted into the close, loving relationship with God that Jesus enjoyed by virtue of being the Son. To be united to Christ is to be empowered and enlightened by the same Holy Spirit that blew upon the waters at creation and descended as a dove upon Jesus at baptism and doesn't just keep his *memory* alive among his followers, but inspires and equips and prompts them to do his work of ministry in the contemporary world. The Trinity, by whatever fallible human words we may describe it, is not just about "them"—Father, Son, and Holy Spirit. The Trinity is about *us*—our relationship with the one God whom we know in three persons, and, based on that, our relationship with one another in the church of Jesus Christ. And *that* is why we celebrate Trinity Sunday—not because it is about some esoteric point of theology, but because it is the mystery in which we are invited to live. It is what lifts us above the status of consumers of religion and makes us members of Christ's body, born for salvation, put to death to the effects of sin, and raised to new life by the Holy Spirit alive and at work within us.

Sometimes I hear people say, sometimes I have thought myself, "Oh, if only I could have lived back in Jesus' time! Faith would be so much easier! To have known the earthly Jesus would have been such a blessing!" In fact, if we *had* lived back in Jesus' time, and had heard him teach, had watched him heal, had received food from his hand, I doubt that faith would have been any easier for us than it was for the people who actually *did* live back in Jesus' time and heard him teach and watched him heal and received food from his hand. By the time Jesus was arrested, according to the Bible, many of his followers had fallen away, had lost interest, had even turned against him. "Oh, but if I had just been there at the cross!" All of the Twelve but one stayed *away* from the cross, went into *hiding*, certainly didn't stand by any of their earlier speculations that Jesus just might be the *Messiah*, just might be the *King*, just might be the *Son of God*. "Oh, but if I could have been there at the empty tomb!" The disciples who *did* go to the tomb were generally perplexed and afraid, and the others who heard about it considered it "an idle tale" (Luke 24:11). No, to have *been* there would not have made us any more faith-filled than the original disciples to whom it appeared that Jesus, arrested and tried and executed and laid in a tomb, was God-forsaken and powerless. We are at no disadvantage to have been born nineteen or twenty centuries after Jesus' death. Indeed, every new generation of faithful reflection and faithful witness and faithful ministry by the church brings us *closer* to a full comprehension not only of who Jesus Christ *was*, but who God—the Father, Son, and Holy Spirit—*is*. If anything, we have a positive *advantage* over those first disciples—*we* have seen the miraculous birth and growth of the church, the body of Christ inspired by the Holy Spirit, even in the most hopeless and discouraging circumstances not only *survive*, but *thrive*. *We* have seen that the church, the body of Christ, not only *exists*, but, by the faithfulness of the Holy Spirit, serves as God's instrument for bringing about and giving witness to the healing and redemption and fullness that God intends for all of creation.

Paul could speak quite confidently about the Trinity—the difference that the crucifixion and resurrection of Christ made in the lives of people who came to *believe* in him, Paul related to our sharing in the glory of God, and to the Holy Spirit powerfully and graciously at work pouring God's own love into our hearts. How else could it be described, this dramatic and wonderful change that came over people, their outlook and their behavior and their affections and their hopes, but an invasion by some invisible presence of God into their soul, bringing about a closeness of relationship and endearment, even with strangers, even across ethnic and national and racial and social and gender lines, who otherwise would be indifferent toward each other, even enemies of each other? How else were they able to work the miracles, large and small, that were happening so often now in the church—forgiveness, healing, generosity, compassion, boldness, courage, transformation? How else were they coming to know God not as some power stern and aloof, menacing and dreadful, but a being kind and merciful, one whom they could rightly address as "Father"? Perhaps we later Christians have become so familiar with the doctrine that we are a little blind to the truth *behind* the words, or have taken the experience of the Trinity for *granted*, and perhaps are not taking full advantage of the fact that the Trinity exists for our benefit and for the sake of the creation that the Trinity cooperated to bring into existence.

Treatises and creeds aside, the Trinity is, and throughout history will remain, a *mystery*. And, like *all* mysteries, including the sacraments, it is *not* to be *explained*, it is to be *experienced*. It is not to be *taught* about or even *talked* about so much as it is to be *lived* in. The *earliest* Christians *knew* that. Before they had a *name* for it, they knew the *reality* of it. They daily lived the *truth* of it, and *because* of that, the church grew and spread and did marvelous things, with miraculous generosity, with miraculous mercy, with miraculous energy, with miraculous love. Their Lord and Savior was not a dead hero, but was alive and at work, and, true to his promise, God sent the Holy Spirit upon the church to inspire it and empower it to carry on the work of Christ that redounded to the glory of the Father. The Creator was not distant from the creation, but deeply caring and personally involved, sending to it his own creative and redeeming agent, the Son, the Word and Wisdom that were with the Father before time began. The Holy Spirit was busy bringing to mind the teaching and example of Christ for new generations of believers in new circumstances, so that the miracles that Jesus did in long-ago Palestine were only *hints* of the miracles *still* to be worked, including the miracles of forgiving and healing and giving and feeding and accepting and comforting and befriending and liberating to be done in and through Spanish Springs Presbyterian Church in Sparks, Nevada.

Are you experiencing the truth of the relationship between the Father, the Son, and the Holy Spirit? Are we experiencing it together—living in the mystery and glorifying God? "Therefore," Paul wrote, "since we are justified by faith, we have peace with God through our Lord Jesus Christ, through whom we have obtained access to this grace in which we stand; and we boast in our hope of sharing the glory of God. And not only that, but we also boast in our sufferings, knowing that suffering produces endurance, and endurance produces character, and character produces hope, and hope does not disappoint us, because God's love has been poured into our hearts through the Holy Spirit that has been given to us" (Rom 5:1–5). When it comes right down to it, that's all we need to know.

Ninth Sunday in Ordinary Time

1 Kings 18:20–39
Galatians 1:1–12
Luke 7:1–10

"Who Is Your God?"

Several years ago, on a tour of the Holy Land, my first visit to Israel/Palestine, one of the first biblical locations we visited was Mount Carmel. According to First Kings, that is where the storied contest between Elijah, the prophet of God, and the four hundred fifty prophets of the Canaanite fertility god Baal and the four hundred prophets of Asherah, Baal's consort, took place. Rather than a single peak, Mount Carmel is actually a mountain range or long ridge, running southeasterly from the Mediterranean Sea toward the Jordan Valley. It forms the southern edge of the Valley of Jezreel, the rich farmland much fought over and fought in during the long history of the Near East. So the Bible doesn't really identify a specific location for the great barbecue cook-off, but the traditional site of the sacrifice is known to the tour guides, though it is not particularly remarkable, and today there are no remnants of the Lord's altar that Elijah rebuilt after King Ahab apparently destroyed it or permitted it to be destroyed and upon which Elijah offered the drenched bull upon which the fire of the Lord fell and "consumed the burnt offering, the wood, the stones, and the dust" (1 Kgs 18:38). There are no charred trees in the place today; the ground is not scorched. It's just a dirt parking lot for tour buses, as I recall. But it is thought to be the site of one of the most dramatic demonstrations of the power and authority of God in the entire Old Testament, written down, scholars tell us, at a time when God's people were taken captive from the Southern Kingdom of Judah and exiled in Babylon and were being tempted there to worship the false god Marduk; the parallels between their present circumstances and the situation in the ancient Northern Kingdom of Israel were dangerously similar. They needed a reminder of how God had demonstrated superiority over the rival Baal for Israel's allegiance. In a time of great drought, when the people's faith in the one true God had wavered, it was God who had delivered life-giving rain to Israel, had made the land fruitful again, had made the ground blossom and flourish, not the idol Baal that was prayed to and sacrificed to and danced for and begged to send what he was actually quite powerless to give.

Long centuries earlier, as the Hebrew people liberated from the ways of empire and slavery and idolatry in Egypt were standing on the brink of the promised land, Moses had instructed them, "Take care that you do not forget the LORD your God, by failing to keep his commandments, his ordinances, and his statutes" (Deut 8:11), and he went on to remind them of God's faithfulness all the way up out of Egypt and through the Sinai and cautioned them how easy it was going to be to forget all that when they found themselves in a land of plenty and turned their attention to what we might summarize as their economic development—building houses, mining precious metals, raising flocks and herds. "If you do forget the LORD your God and follow other gods to serve and worship them, I solemnly warn you today that you shall surely perish" (8:19). And when, after Moses died, Joshua his successor led the people across the Jordan and into the promised land, he had commanded them to revere the Lord and serve the Lord in sincerity and in faithfulness and to put away the gods their ancestors had served in the land of empire with its habits of materialism and its ideals of domination and its methods of slavery and its trust in weapons, "and serve the LORD. If you are unwilling to serve the LORD, choose this day whom you will serve, whether the gods your ancestors served in the region beyond the River or the gods of the Amorites in whose land you are living; but as for me and my household, we will serve the LORD" (Josh 24:14c–15). And the people had responded, "Far be it from us that we should forsake the LORD to serve other gods. . . . [W]e also will serve the LORD, for he is our God" (24:16b, 18b). But, of course, they *did* forsake the Lord, and many times over, generation after generation, and that is what resulted in the ultimate destruction of Israel the Northern Kingdom by Assyria and the people of Judah, the Southern Kingdom, being taken into exile in Babylon, where they encountered the worship of Marduk the ancient god of Mesopotamia and a whole constellation of lesser deities.

Of course, as Israel's theologians came to discern over time, it wasn't really a matter of choosing between multiple divine beings. Baal couldn't set fire to his prophets' sacrifice of a bull because Baal didn't really exist. Baal wasn't just an *inferior* god; Baal wasn't a god *at all*. Likewise, *Marduk* didn't really exist. It wasn't *Marduk* who had created heaven and earth, and the first chapter of Genesis was written to set the record straight for the captives who might be tempted to think otherwise. The only God in all the universe was and is the God of Abraham and Sarah, Isaac and Rebekah, Jacob and Rachel, Jesus and Mary and Joseph and Peter and Paul. Biblical scholars observe, and biblical archaeology seems to confirm, that it wasn't so much that King Ahab had turned from the true God to the impostor Baal, but that he hadn't denied the claims being made for Baal, hadn't unequivocally declared that God alone was God. The king of Israel, yielding to the preference of his wife Jezebel, had tolerated the cult of Baal and perhaps participated in it himself from time to time without staking his throne on the truth of monotheism, to use a more recent term. And, so, the people of Israel had *likewise* neglected to take an unequivocal oath, had refused to stake their future on God and God's promises alone. The prophets of Baal could have danced and sacrificed all day long, but all their frenzy wasn't going to bring rain, because Baal didn't really exist, wasn't any sort of god at all.

Centuries later, when Paul wrote his stern letter to the churches of Galatia, a region of what is now Turkey, the issue was more subtle. The God who manifested himself in Jesus of Nazareth—did he require circumcision before he could be rightly worshiped and relied upon, as some itinerant preachers were claiming, and imposing other qualifications that tended to entrust salvation to their own purity rather than faith in the death and resurrection of Christ? As there is but one God, so there is but one gospel, Paul explained—the gospel Paul proclaimed to the Galatians that he had received through a revelation of Jesus Christ himself, and which was not for the Jews only but for the Gentiles as well, conditioned not on an outward circumcision but working a circumcision of the heart, based not on a taste or preference among multiple possibilities of doctrine but upon the person of Jesus Christ, crucified for his obedience to the only one true God and then resurrected for his obedience to the only one true God, living, empowering, forgiving, granting life everlasting.

There are, of course, no other gods, though we are tempted to worship other would-be truths, sacrificing to them, even, our treasure, our allegiance, ultimately our souls. In fact, daily, we succumb to them in some degree, alongside our worship, our offerings, our professed allegiance to God. Like the Hebrews of old, professing allegiance to God alone when they were rallied by Joshua to do so, we make solemn declaration of our faith in God, but, in daily living, we often neglect to choose between the God we know in Jesus Christ and the god-like claims of the economy, of partisan politics, of nationalism, of racism, of consumerism, of me-ism, many of which masquerade as good and wise and pious. We wouldn't think of worshiping Marduk or Baal or the gods of Egypt, but we often credit the claims that are still being made for them thousands of years after their altars and temples fell into ruin. Or, worse, maybe, we worship *ourselves*, trust ultimately our own wits and accomplishments as the highest authority, place our desires at the center of the universe and rationalize them in so many ways, and create for ourselves a heaven from which we exclude even those whom God said are his especial concern and whom Jesus taught must therefore be our especial concern as well. What Paul was criticizing among the Galatians was, it seems, the very sort of exclusionary legalism for which he had once prided himself and upon which he had, he admitted, quite erroneously staked his salvation. He came to understand that his law-keeping gave him no better claim upon salvation than the most wretched sinner, much less people who were different from him in race, nationality, language, or circumstance.

The great hazard tempting us from allegiance to God today is not Baal or Marduk or any other idol of wood or stone, though similar cults and paganisms still exist. Rather, it is the vague spirituality that seems so readily to accommodate secularism and materialism and nationalism and ethnism, to coin a word, and a politics that easily surrenders integrity of spirit to base instinct and demagoguery. But Baal never has been able, and still is not able, to produce rain. And salvation never has been worked, and still cannot be worked, by following or imposing rules. "Faith alone!" the sixteenth-century Protestant Reformers rightly confessed, and then too often went on to scrutinize the minutiae of each other's doctrine and behavior in ways that established an entire pantheon of virtual claimants for religious allegiance. And our reforming ancestors didn't have near the array of material and consumerist seductions that are wooing us all today away from single-minded and single-hearted trust in God.

One of the manifold reasons for regular—at least weekly—corporate worship of God, I think, is that it places us in the situation of being reminded of Joshua's question to the people who had pledged allegiance to the God who repeatedly had shown himself to *be* God. "Choose this day whom you will serve" (24:15), he commanded them. "The Lord our God we will serve, and him we will obey" (24:24), they responded. And then, a later generation, living under the same covenant, only turned back to the God whom they had betrayed by lavishing their allegiance and affections upon Baal, who was not a god at all, when they saw that Baal was powerless to send fire upon his own altar despite all the antics of his prophets, but that "the fire of the Lord fell and consumed the burnt offering, the wood, the stones, and the dust, and even licked up the water that was in the trench" (1 Kgs 18:38). It was then that they fell on their faces and said, 'The Lord indeed is God; the Lord indeed is God'" (18:39).

There is no other God. There is no other ultimate authority. There is no greater power. There is no other so worthy of allegiance and trust and loving obedience. And this one true God has raised his Son from the tomb, vindicating Jesus' faith in him and our faith in Jesus. There is no comparable truth. And we *attest* that truth, we give *witness* to it, every time we come together to find our place again in the shadow of his cross, listen again to the words that he spoke, hear again the commandments by which he lived, confess again that he is Lord of our lives, eat and drink again and find him alive in the midst of our gathering, and again offer him our treasure, our loyalty, our love. And chief of those commandments by which he lived is this: "I am the Lord your God, who brought you out of the land of Egypt, out of the house of slavery; you shall have no other gods before me" (Exod 20:2–3). And, as Jesus attested, the most important way in which that commandment is observed is to love the Lord our God with all of one's heart, with all of one's soul, with all of one's strength, and with all of one's mind, and to love one's neighbor as oneself. What room can that leave to worship, to sacrifice to, to give allegiance to, any other god?

To keep the office of daily prayer—that is, to hear the words of scripture and to offer God prayers at set times each day—as Christian communities have done for centuries, is not only for *God's* sake, giving what is God's due. It is also for *our* sake, helping to keep us mindful of God, to keep us mindful that there is only *one* God, to keep us mindful that this one and only God is the God proclaimed in scripture and demonstrated in the life, death, and resurrection of Jesus Christ. It is so vitally important to worship God regularly, at least weekly, not only because that is what God *deserves*, but because we need the *reminder* of God, lest we give in to the voices that claim there are other gods to be worshiped and obeyed and sacrificed to and that shout and cajole and whisper in our ears and our minds and, perhaps, our hearts, weekly, daily, hourly. Listening to scripture read, voicing our prayers alone and in unison, yes, and confessing God's faithfulness, making an offering to God from and in acknowledgment of the bounty God has bestowed upon us, eating together with and in remembrance of Jesus Christ, singing above the self-centered din of the pride and lust and greed championed by the persistent cults of Baal and Marduk and all the other gods that are not God—and coming together for each other's support in living and loving the truth of God—that is our testimony that all the ranting and raving of the prophets of Baal and the rest cannot bring down fire from heaven or work any other magic, simply because Baal is no god at all.

Who is your God? Your presence here today gives witness that you have pledged to turn away from the worship of all that is *not* God but, instead, turn all your heart and all your soul and all your strength and all your mind to the one who alone is God and, therefore, also, to love your neighbor as yourself.

Tenth Sunday in Ordinary Time
Spanish Springs Presbyterian Church, Sparks, Nevada
June 6, 2010

1 Kings 17:8–24
Galatians 1:11–24
Luke 7:11–17

"Crossing Boundaries"

I was reminded by the current issue of *Smithsonian* magazine that this summer marks the fiftieth anniversary of a book that became one of my favorite motion pictures, *To Kill a Mockingbird*. Harper Lee's novel and the movie that came from it tell in masterful style a number of stories, really, but the overall framework is the decision of attorney Atticus Finch to defend a black man against a charge of raping a white woman in the segregated South—a charge that the audience understands from the evidence to be patently false. Gregory Peck's portrayal of the courageous attorney won him an Academy Award. But the *true* award, the more *important* one, goes to those people in real life who, in small ways and large, defied the customs and prejudices of era and place to make a witness about dignity and justice and hope. The theme has been repeated over time and in one way or another in Germany and Holland, in South Africa, in India, perhaps in your own school or your own business or your own club or your own church, whenever and wherever people have been bold enough, faithful enough, to follow their conscience—what people of faith would call the leading of the Holy Spirit—and ignore the boundaries that have been erected to separate people, to provide an excuse for disregarding the image of God in people.

The general ignorance of geography and disinterest in history in recent generations have prevented a lot of readers of the Bible from identifying certain clues that the biblical writers used to convey their message about the scope and power of God's grace. It is easy for moderns to lump all ancient people and faraway places into a foggy antiquity and indistinct foreignness. But if we don't think that the place names and nationalities mentioned in scripture matter very much, we will miss, for instance, much of the extraordinary claim that the writer of First Kings was making when he told the story of the prophet Elijah and the widow of Zarephath.

At the beginning of chapter 17 of First Kings, we meet Elijah the Tishbite, from the town of Tishbe in Gilead, who confronted Ahab the king with the declaration, "As the LORD God of Israel lives, before whom I stand, there shall be neither dew nor rain these years, except by my word" (1 Kgs 17:1). And the Lord then directed Elijah the Tishbite to a brook, the Wadi Cherith, east of the Jordan River, where, during the period of drought that he had announced, he was fed by ravens who brought him bread and meat in the morning and bread and meat in the evening, and he drank water from the wadi, while others in the region went hungry and thirsty. This is the Bible's first mention of Elijah, the prophet who became such a prominent figure in the Old Testament and, by frequent reference, even in the *New* Testament— the New Testament writers, and Luke especially, saw in Elijah a forerunner of Christ. Many of the things Jesus did are told within a narrative framework intended to highlight the *similarities* between Jesus' ministry and that of Elijah, who came so many centuries before him, and to *interpret* what *Jesus* did in the light of what *Elijah* did.

Tishbe, Elijah's hometown, was in the portion of the Northern Kingdom of Israel that lay just on the eastern bank of the Jordan River. Ahab was king of the Northern Kingdom at that time, and the Bible informs us that he was dominated by his wife Jezebel, who was a Phoenician, a worshiper of Baal, the god of the Canaanites who had inhabited the entire area before the Israelites moved in. Officially, Yahweh, the God of Abraham and Isaac and Jacob, was the only deity in whom the people were to put their trust, and whom they were to worship, but the old cult of Baal survived in pockets here and there and, in the ninth century BC, was gaining in strength. Baal was a god of *fertility*, which meant that the *worship* of Baal was associated with *rain*. But the fertility part meant that the Baal religion featured cultic prostitution and other sexual indulgences. Probably through the influence of his wife, Ahab the king built a *house* for Baal—a *temple*—in his capital city of Samaria and erected there an *altar* to the Canaanite god.

It was this whole situation, or in anticipation of it, that Elijah the prophet of Yahweh confronted when he announced to Ahab that the *true* God who had *real* control of the rain and everything else was going to shut up the heavens and bring drought upon the land, which would lead to famine. The next several chapters demonstrate a contest between the true God,

Israel's God, the God represented by Elijah, and the false god Baal, the idol championed by Jezebel, culminating in the great competition to see which deity had the power to light the fire of an altar to make a burnt offering. And the prophets of *Baal* called upon *their* god to send down fire and none came, but *Elijah* called upon *his* God to send down fire and *Elijah's* God *did*.

The Bible tells not only of a *contest* between the deities. It also tells of a *contrast*. "Then the word of the Lord came to [Elijah], saying, 'Go now to Zarephath, which belongs to Sidon, and live there; for I have commanded a widow there to feed you.' So [Elijah] set out and went to Zarephath" (17:8–10a). Now Sidon was a city in *Phoenicia*, an *important* city, and the very place from which Jezebel, the Baal-worshiping wife of Israel's king Ahab, had come. Jezebel was the princess of the Sidonians—her father was their king. Sidon and the region around it were the center of the cult of Baal, the Canaanite fertility god. Only things hadn't been going very well for the homeland of Baal-worship. The region was caught in the grip of the drought that Elijah had announced to Ahab, and, with the lack of rain, famine had come upon the land—the very land where all sorts of sacrifices were being made to Baal as the god of fertility, of plant-life and growth and harvest.

Zarephath lay just a few miles south of Sidon and was a port city famous for exporting grain and wine and olive oil. Only now, there would have been no grain or wine or oil to export. "When [Elijah] came to the gate of the town, a widow was there gathering sticks; he called to her and said, 'Bring me a little water in a vessel, so that I may drink'" (17:10b). Clean water would have been precious during that time of drought, but ancient Near Eastern rules of hospitality meant that Elijah, the guest, would have been entitled to whatever water the woman had. "As she was going to bring it, [Elijah] called to her and said, 'Bring me a morsel of bread in your hand'" (17:11). While the people of Zarephath had been trying to stretch what little food they had, Elijah had been feasting on bread and meat brought to him by ravens—birds, by the way, that Jews considered unclean, and therefore no respectable Jew should have any contact with, dead or alive, but here, God had no scruples about using what famously righteous people considered to be unclean and to keep his own prophet alive, and Elijah had no scruples about receiving from them the food that he needed to *stay* alive. How insensitive Elijah's request must have seemed to the woman, whose life as a widow would have been hard enough *before* the drought. She had no food to spare. But, again, the rules of hospitality were paramount even over her own survival and the survival of her son. "She said [to Elijah], 'As the Lord your God lives, I have nothing baked, only a handful of meal in a jar, and a little oil in a jug; I am now gathering a couple of sticks, so that I may go home and prepare it for myself and my son, that we may eat it, and die'"

(17:12). To this, Elijah replied, essentially, almost as if he hadn't heard what the woman said, "Okay, you go ahead and do that. But first, make some for *me*."

The cupboard was bare—the handful of meal, the little bit of oil, were all that she had left. After that, she and her son must surely starve, as others were starving around her. *Her* god, Baal, the god of fertility to whom prayers had been raised and sacrifices had been offered and for whom acts of cultic prostitution had been performed, had failed to stock the grocery stores. "Elijah"—the prophet of the one *true* God, worshiped across the border in Israel but in fact the creator and ruler of the whole universe, the God who *truly* has control of rain and the whole rest of nature—"said to [the woman], 'Do not be afraid; go and do as you have said; but first make me a little cake of it and bring it to me'"—as the rules of hospitality required—"'and afterwards make something for yourself and your son. For thus says the Lord the God of Israel: The jar of meal and the jug of oil will not fail until the day that the Lord sends rain on the earth.' She went and did as Elijah said, so that she as well as he and her household ate for many days" (17:13–15).

Did you hear the words "so that"? By doing what the prophet of Israel's God said, the woman was given what was needed for life. "The jar of meal was not emptied, neither did the jug of oil fail according to the word of the Lord that he spoke by Elijah" (17:16). As God had caused the drought to serve God's purpose, so God eventually sent the rain. The scenario permitted a Baal-worshiping woman of a foreign nation to survive the drought as an instance of God's grace that knows no boundaries, a bountiful blessing that is not just for *Jew* but for *Phoenician* as well—not just for the *believer*, but even for the *non*-believer. And when, having survived the drought and the famine, the woman's only son fell deathly ill, and she supposed that the presence of Elijah, this man of God, the powerful God of Israel, had brought the calamity upon her house by drawing God's attention to her and thus to her sins, whatever they might have been, and the boy was dead or as good as dead, Elijah called upon God to bring the breath of life back into the boy, and God did, and "the woman said to Elijah, 'Now I know that you are a man of God, and that the word of the Lord in your mouth is truth'" (17:24). Presumably, having witnessed a miracle that addressed her profound grief, she became a believer in the God of Israel.

The day that Jesus appeared in the synagogue at Nazareth and read from the scroll of the prophet Isaiah where it says,

> "The Spirit of the Lord is upon me,
>   because he has anointed me
>   to bring good news to the poor.

> He has sent me to proclaim release to the captives
> and recovery of sight to the blind,
> to let the oppressed go free,
> to proclaim the year of the Lord's favor" (Luke 4:18–19)

and then said to the people gathered in the synagogue, "Today this scripture has been fulfilled in your hearing" (4:21b), and he detected that they were thinking critically that he ought to be performing in his *own hometown* the healing miracles that he had instead been performing *elsewhere*, Jesus recalled the miracle of the meal and oil in the widow's kitchen in Zarephath. "'Truly I tell you, no prophet is accepted in the prophet's hometown. But the truth is, there were many widows in *Israel* in the time of Elijah, when the heaven was shut up for three years and six months, and there was severe famine over all the land; yet Elijah was sent to none of *them* except to a widow at *Zarephath* in *Sidon*'" (4:24–26). He also recalled that it was not *Israelite* lepers that Elijah's successor, Elisha, had cured of their disease, but the leper Naaman, a Syrian general, a non-Jew. "When they heard this, all in the synagogue were filled with rage. They got up, drove him out of the town, and led him to the brow of the hill on which their town was built, so that they might hurl him off the cliff" (4:28–29). But he managed to escape the mob "and went on his way" (4:30b). And, in our Gospel reading today, Jesus, after having cured a Roman centurion's slave (but from a distance, because the centurion, whose house it would have been forbidden a Jew to enter anyway, said that he was not worthy to have Jesus as his houseguest), healed the son of a widow who lived in a town on the Phoenician border. Like the son of the widow of Zarephath, this boy was the woman's only son (so that his death would have presented an economic crisis for the woman as well as an emotional one). He was dead, or was assumed to be so—was already being carried out from the town for burial. As Elijah had once met the widow of Zarephath at the city gate, now Jesus met the widow of Nain at the city gate. "When the Lord saw her, he had compassion for her and said to her, 'Do not weep'" (7:13). He knew nothing of her faith, apparently—living in a Galilean bordertown, she might well have been a *Gentile* who did not believe in the God of *Israel*. Despite that, Jesus commanded the boy to rise up, and the boy indeed "sat up and began to speak, and Jesus gave him to his mother" (7:15)—the same words used in the story of Elijah and the widow of Zarephath.

Time after time in the Bible, the God who made the world is shown to have no regard for the lines that human beings draw on maps, has no regard for the differences that human beings use to excuse oppression and injustice, has no regard for social conventions that result in exclusion or rejection.

The God alongside whose *authority Baal* is proved to be *powerless* is also the God alongside whose *mercy* the *intolerant* are shown to be *unfaithful*. In the words and deeds of the prophets, boundaries of uncleanness and propriety, whether in the form of accepting food from ravens or venturing into the territory of idol-worshipers or lodging with a widow, are crossed to suit God's purpose. In the words and deeds and resurrection of his Son, God crosses even the boundary of *death*, vindicating the love and mercy and faith that revealed God's will of fullness of life in even the most hopeless situation. In choosing Paul the persecutor to spread the gospel to the Greeks and the Romans, the Lord even crossed the boundary of worn-out interpretations of the law. What boundaries is God in Jesus Christ calling *us* to cross, in order to work miracles of salvation?

Eleventh Sunday in Ordinary Time

Spanish Springs Presbyterian Church, Sparks, Nevada

June 10, 2007

1 Kings 21:1–21a
Galatians 2:15–21
Luke 7:36—8:3

"Holier Than Jesus?"

From a distance of two thousand years and an entire gospel of forgiveness, you and I may not quite understand the shock and dismay that must have permeated that dining room when the guests and their host noticed that a *prostitute* had entered the room and had caressed Jesus' feet. Very likely, there were *others* present in the room or in the courtyard outside who had not been invited to the dinner party—such events were a big deal in a village like Capernaum, which, presumably, is where this incident took place. You couldn't very well keep a dinner party private in small-town Palestine, and if people had been hearing about Jesus' cures and exorcisms, it is natural that some of them wanted to see for *themselves* what was going on at the house of Simon the Pharisee. The guests and their host would have been reclining on the floor, leaning on an elbow, eating food that was placed on a low table or mat in front of them, their legs and feet stretched out behind them.

Jesus might have been as startled as *anyone* when he first felt a drop of oil or ointment on his feet, though it would not have been at all unusual for the *host* to have instructed his *servants* to bathe or anoint the feet of his *guests*. But this was not ointment—at least *not yet*. It was a *tear*—the tear of a woman regarded as unsuitable to be in the company of respectable men, or in the company of *anyone* respectable, in fact. And she not only had the audacity to come right into the room, apparently intending to anoint Jesus' feet, but when she began crying instead, she let fall her hair—again, something that no respectable woman would do in public—and used it to wipe his feet dry. Everybody must have been looking at her by this time, and at *Jesus*, who just lay there letting her do it! Simon the Pharisee had invited Jesus to dinner out of respect for him, thinking him to be perhaps a prophet, based on his teaching and his miracles. But he was no *true* prophet, Simon decided, if he didn't even know what sort of a woman was caressing his feet, and, if he was at all religiously inclined, he certainly wouldn't have let a woman of *her* reputation touch him! She was unclean, according to the law, and for her to touch *Jesus* made *him* unclean according to the law, as well. Just because it's in the Bible, let us not miss the indications that this was a very erotic, or at least sensual, incident—a harlot massaging Jesus' feet with her hair! So, Simon the Pharisee must have thought, it was *true* what people had been gossiping about Jesus—he *was* a friend of tax collectors and sinners!

Yes, that *was* true. But it was *also* true that Jesus was a *prophet*, and *more* than a prophet. Not only could he tell what people were *thinking*—like what Simon was thinking just then. He exercised the authority to *forgive sins*—something that no prophet would have dared to do. And what was true *then* is still true *now*, and, when people really understand that, it tends to cause just the same sort of scandal *now* as it did *then*.

As Jesus glanced around the room, he could not have missed the look of surprise and disgust on the faces of the people gathered there as the woman continued kissing his feet and anointing them with the ointment she had brought. "Jesus spoke up and said to [his host], 'Simon, I have something to say to you.' 'Teacher,' he replied, 'Speak.' 'A certain creditor had two debtors; one owed five hundred denarii, and the other fifty. When they could not pay, he canceled the debts for both of them. Now which of them will love him more?'" (Luke 7:40–42). Riddles were a common form of entertainment at parties and at the dinner table in Jesus' time—the host and guests would match wits and wisdom as a part of the evening's repartee. Still astonished at what he was seeing, though, Simon might not have been at the top of his form just then. Or maybe he sensed that *he* was going to become an *object* lesson. "Simon answered, 'I suppose the one for whom he canceled the greater debt.' And Jesus said to him, 'You have judged rightly'" (7:43). At least Simon had gotten *something* right. But did he understand the implications for the social situation unfolding in his own dining room? "'Do you see this woman?'" (7:44b) Jesus asked—not "prostitute," not "harlot," not "sinner," but "*woman*." "'I entered *your* house; *you* gave me no water for my feet, but *she* has bathed my feet with her *tears* and dried them with her *hair*. *You* gave me no kiss, but from the time I came in *she* has not stopped kissing my *feet*. *You* did not anoint my head with oil, but *she* has anointed my *feet* with ointment'" (7:44c–46). The righteous man, the Pharisee, had extended none of the little courtesies that, if not exactly *required* on such occasions, still might have been *expected* of a host offering hospitality to his invited guests. Now came the most shocking part of the episode. "'Therefore, I tell you, *her* sins, which were *many*, have been *forgiven*; hence she has shown great love. But the one to whom *little* is forgiven, *loves* little.' Then [Jesus] said to her, 'Your sins are forgiven.' . . . And he said to the woman, 'Your faith has saved you; go in peace'" (7:47–48, 50).

Jesus' ready forgiveness of the woman's sins stirred up considerable comment among the dinner party. It *ought* to stir up considerable discussion among *us*. Her sins seem to have been in a class that Christians for centuries have considered somehow especially bad—sexual—and, as far as the text is concerned, she hadn't even voiced words of confession or words of repentance. Instead, in the eyes of those present—all but one, that is— she had even on that very occasion *compounded* her sinful unworthiness by committing yet *another* lewd and disreputable act. But Jesus read in her deed not *lust*, but *love*—purer and more freely given than his host or any of the *invited* guests had shown. She probably couldn't have explained her deeds in terms of theology, not even in the classic language of simple piety. "Messiah," "Son of God," "First-born of all creation"—these terms were not in her vocabulary. She only knew what was brimming up in her eyes and overflowing in her heart, perhaps from a pardon already pronounced, or a healing previously worked, or a word of comforting truth uttered, or a kind smile turned her way. And Jesus pronounced her clean, acceptable, worthy, made right with God, *forgiven*, by the mixture of love and faith that prompted her to render spontaneously such an un-self-conscious act of pure devotion. The barrier of uncleanness was dissolved by the holy touch of Jesus, or, in this case, by touching the holiness of Jesus with a gesture of immense gratitude. Luke doesn't tell us what happened during the remainder of the dinner party. Did Simon the Pharisee get the point and ask Jesus to forgive *him*? Did Simon's guests get up and leave in disgust, perhaps *run* in disgust to the nearest rabbi to ask how to become clean again *themselves*, who had been in the presence of such a breach not just of social etiquette, but religious law? Did Jesus get up and excuse himself, leaving them to grumble and gossip and judge themselves to be *holier* than Jesus, whom scriptures and we declare to be the Son of God?

The Bible knows of no greater gauge of how people feel about each other than whether they will dine with each other. Think of the elder son in the story of the prodigal, how he refused to go into his father's house and join the dinner party that was being thrown in his younger brother's honor. It had been a great victory for the inclusiveness of the gospel when Peter the apostle had sat down in Antioch to eat at the same table with the *Gentiles* whom Paul had won to the Christian faith. No food should be judged unclean, as he had learned in an earlier vision from God, and so no one who refused to keep the Jewish dietary laws should be excluded from Peter's ministry, even Peter's companionship at the dinner table. Peter, the stubborn Jew, had defied and ignored the law's barrier that had been destroyed by the cross of Jesus Christ. But then some Christians of Jewish background came to Antioch on a visit from the conservative church at Jerusalem and complained loudly that Peter was violating the law and compromising the faith by eating with Gentiles, and so Peter quit the practice himself and apparently forbade *any other Jewish* Christians to mix socially with *Gentile* Christians.

Paul was *disappointed*, and then *chagrined*, and then *enraged* that the converts he had won to Jesus Christ would be treated by fellow believers as second-class Christians. Not only that, but it raised the question of just *whose* faithfulness has *saved* us—our *own* faithfulness, faithfulness to *rules* and *regulations*? Certainly not! Paul declared. The faithfulness that *saves* us—has *already* saved us—is the faithfulness of Jesus Christ *himself* in obediently surrendering to the *cross*. We are not justified, not rectified, not "made right" with God, Paul said, by anything that *we* can do—not even by following the law perfectly, on dietary matters or anything else—but only through *Christ's* faithful death for our sake. "I died to the law" (Gal 2:19), Paul wrote to the Gentile churches of Galatia, who were being pressed by the conservatives to be circumcised and to eat only what the law of Moses said to eat. "I *died* to the *law*, so that I might *live* to *God*. I have been crucified with Christ; and it is no longer *I* who live, but it is *Christ* who lives *in me*. And the life I now live in the *flesh* I live by faith in the *Son of God*, who loved me and gave himself for me. I do not nullify the grace of God"(2:19–21a)—in other words, Paul was saying, I don't treat Christ's death as being of no importance by staking *my* salvation on *my* ability to follow the *rules* and *regulations*. "If justification comes through the *law*, then Christ died for nothing" (2:21b). And any rules or regulations that would *categorize* people, and so *divide* them as between worthy and unworthy, clean and unclean, proper dinner companions or *not* proper dinner companions, must *fall* alongside the reconciling reality of the cross of Jesus Christ. For in Christ, there is neither male nor female, Jew nor Greek, slave nor free, nor any other distinction that may grab headlines and rock church councils and prompt some to draw lines distinguishing who is "in" and who is "out" and who is a real Christian and who regrettably is only going through the motions but not following all the rules that we who are "in" pride *ourselves* on being able to follow. And certainly there can be no *halfway* Christianity, in which people are commended for having confessed faith and trust in Jesus Christ, but are nevertheless denied full participation in the church and are excluded from our friendship.

The supreme mark of God's *righteousness* is God's *forgiveness* of sinners without their having *earned* God's forgiveness. The supreme mark of Christ's *faithfulness* was Christ's *willingness* to touch what was *unholy* with his own holy love and holy mercy and holy obedience—even the unholiness of the outcast and the despised, even the unholiness of the cross of gruesome torture and execution, even the unholiness of death and the grave. Who among us dares to reckon him- or herself as holier than Jesus? What believer, what congregation, what denomination could refuse to welcome, befriend, and associate with *anyone* who loves Jesus Christ and trusts in Jesus Christ and desires to serve Jesus Christ? We are all one in Christ, the gospel declares. Paul must have been truly dismayed at how his uncircumcised, feast-loving Gentile converts were not considered good enough to eat at the same table as *other* Christians—how they were being told, in essence, that they must be holier than Jesus.

In 1994, a bloody civil war raged in the African nation of Rwanda. Tribal hatred set Hutus against Tutsis, and Tutsis were slaughtered by the thousands. At one town, a group of 13,500 *Christians*, both Hutus and Tutsis, had gathered together for refuge despite their tribal distinctions and their denominational differences. Some were Anglicans, some Roman Catholics, some Pentecostals, some Baptists, some members of other denominations. When the paramilitary militias came to the village, the soldiers ordered the Hutu and Tutsi Christians to separate themselves according to tribe, so that the Tutsis could be killed and the Hutus spared. The people refused to segregate themselves, declaring to the soldiers that they were all one in Christ. For that, they were *all* killed, gunned down en masse and their bodies dumped into trenches. The soldiers committed a despicable act, but the Rwandan Christians made a profound witness. The truth of the gospel, the refugees knew, was that they had already been "crucified with Christ"; out of obedience to the truth of the gospel, they surrendered their earthly lives rather than deny the grace of God that had made all of them, without distinction, *one* in *Christ*.

Are people saved by their *own* holiness, perhaps holiness more pure and uncompromising even than that shown by Christ? Or are people saved by the holiness of *Christ*—holiness that welcomes and embraces what others call "unclean," holiness that receives and sanctifies gestures of love and deeds of faith, holiness that shows its authenticity by stooping down to touch the *unholy* and that finds its purpose in mercy unearned and even unasked for? The church of Jesus Christ finds *its* holiness by faithfully following its Lord, who *welcomes* the faithful love of even those whom society reckons most despised and unworthy. Rejoice! That means that sinners like you and me, surely, have a place in the church of Jesus Christ, who is happy to share his table with us.

Twelfth Sunday in Ordinary Time

Spanish Springs Presbyterian Church, Sparks, Nevada

June 20, 2010

1 Kings 19:1–15a
Galatians 3:23–29
Luke 8:26–39

"God in Real Time"

Once upon a time long ago, well before texting, well before the internet, well before the printing press, even generations before the invention of writing, perhaps, the people of Israel sat around the campfire, sat around the table, sat around the marketplace, and told stories of God—stories of God's creation of the world and the stars above it and the seas beneath it, stories of God's interaction with individuals and the communities they led, stories about how God made and kept promises. Eventually, those stories were written down, when it seemed especially important that they be preserved lest they be forgotten. And, in time, those writings came to be considered sacred, and they were collected and bound together as the scriptures. Eventually, *Christians* added to the scriptures *their* collections of stories and sayings of Jesus and letters that had been written to encourage and correct congregations of followers of Christ, which likewise had been preserved lest *they* be forgotten, often in the process of addressing contemporary debates and disturbances within particular congregations.

Some of the stories told of some pretty spectacular events—unprecedented floods, a dry escape route through the heart of the sea, the sun made to stand still in the sky; water turned suddenly to wine, blindness being replaced by sight, even the dead walking out of their tombs. But most of those huddled around the campfire or feasting at the dinner table or lingering in the marketplace, most of those gathered around the baptismal font and the communion table and the lectern, had not themselves witnessed worlds being formed or the sea being parted or astronomical oddities, nor even a star shining brightly over a birthplace or waves being calmed with a word or a new city descending from on high. But there was enough in their own experience of God, and of God in Christ, and of the powerful presence of the Holy Spirit, that all the great things told of in the stories seemed not only plausible but fully in keeping with the God whom they had come to know and trust. Were it not so, the stories would have died out long before they were considered worthy of being committed to writing. Were it not so, the people who considered them to be sacred would not have perceived parallels between the events of old and the contemporary wonders of which they themselves were a part, in which they themselves found comfort and courage and hope.

And they did just that, though some of them perhaps needed help to detect in their own experience the footprints of God. In our own day, though, the Bible seems like a closed book to many people, more a tale of magic than a testimony to miracle. On the other hand, a lot of folk who passionately argue that the stories in the scriptures are factual in every detail don't seem to think that God is active in the same way now as in biblical times. We twenty-first-century people of God may stand more in need even than the people of old who were actually *living* in some of those places mentioned in scripture, who still felt *threatened* by some of the nations spoken of in the Bible, who were not yet *habituated* into demanding scientific explanations for every departure from the ordinary, of recognizing that our *own* stories are a *continuation* of God's interaction with people of faith. Thanks to Cecil B. DeMille and others, some of us may think that, in order for it to be *God's* doing, it has to be a spectacular event of blockbuster proportions. And as a matter of fact, we can now create a lot of that for ourselves with computer graphics.

But consider the stories in our scripture passages this morning. Who among us, discouraged by the unbelief around us, and having gone out of our way to perform some deed that we felt God wanted us to do, hasn't experienced the miracle of receiving new strength to persevere and new resolve to be obedient? Who among us, having been faced with a decision between accepting the unhealthy status quo and risking the consequences of changing a situation that seemed contrary to God's will, hasn't ended up receiving the courage to choose the more difficult path of trying to right the wrong? The vast majority of us will never see anyone stretch out his or her hand and the ocean deep open up to allow our escape from a pursuing army. We will probably never ourselves witness someone commanding raging waves to be calm and suddenly they are. But at some point, we will be eager to sense God's approval, and a new opportunity of service will present itself; we will know someone whose life is a torment and realize that by daring to name the demons at the cost of upsetting the comfortable familiar, that by daring not to compromise with the customary evils, we might be an instrument to set that child of God free to live life in joy and gratitude. And so God is at work today in the world God loves, healing, liberating, restoring, just as God was active in biblical times, and great heroes of God's work of salvation are present right here among us, not just confined to the pages of the Bible, scarcely conscious of their crucial role in the remarkable story of salvation, people of everyday faith to whom future generations of the faithful will point and say, "Surely we can perceive that God was at work through them."

Elijah the prophet had triumphed in his contest with the prophets of Baal. Fire fell from heaven upon the sacrificial altar he had prepared "and consumed the burnt offering, the wood, the stones, and the dust, and even licked up the water that was in the trench" (1 Kgs 18:38), and "when the people saw it"—the people who *should* have been worshiping the God of *Israel* but had *lapsed* into their idolatrous ways of *Baal*-worship—"they fell on their faces and said, 'The LORD indeed is God; the LORD indeed is God'" (18:39b), and at Elijah's instruction, they seized the prophets of Baal and slaughtered them—the false prophets whose pitiful appeal to Baal to set fire to *their* sacrifice had gone unanswered. But when Baal's patroness Jezebel, queen of the Northern Kingdom of Israel, heard about it, she swore that she would track Elijah down and kill him. She sent her messenger to Elijah to deliver the threat, and despite the impressive demonstration of God's mighty power over Baal and Baal's agents that Elijah himself had arranged, the prophet fled, terrified, into the wilderness beyond Beersheba. Beersheba was the farthest place you could go and still be in the land God had given to the Israelites. There he collapsed, frightened and despondent, under a broom tree.

Elijah asked God to end his life, so hopeless did he think things were. After all, he knew, persecution and execution were too often the earthly rewards for prophets. Instead, God provided food and water (as God had provided food and water for Elijah on a previous occasion when he had fled from a royal threat). An angel of the Lord said to him, "'Get up and eat, otherwise the journey will be too much for you'" (19:7b). (Do you hear a prefiguring of how *communion* is Christ's gift intended to be received regularly as sustenance for us on our *own* journey of faith?) "[Elijah] got up, and ate and drank; then he went in the strength of that food forty days and forty nights to Horeb, the mount of God" (19:8)—the very same mountain where Moses had once spent forty days and forty nights with God.

"At that place he came to a cave"—was it the same cleft of rock in which God had shielded Moses from his glory when he passed by?—"and spent the night there. Then the word of the LORD came to him, saying, 'What are you doing here, Elijah?'" (19:9). "Why are you—my prophet whom I have called and empowered, my prophet who has already demonstrated my superiority over Baal and his champions—why are you whimpering in the dark instead of proclaiming my message of freedom and my deeds of salvation?"

> "Go out and stand on the mountain before the LORD, for the LORD is about to pass by." Now there was a great wind, so strong that it was splitting mountains and breaking rocks in pieces before the LORD, but the LORD was not in the wind; and after the wind an earthquake, but the LORD was not in the earthquake; and after the earthquake a fire, but the LORD was not in the fire; and after the fire a sound of sheer silence. When Elijah heard it, he wrapped his face in his mantle and went out and stood at the entrance of the cave. Then there came a voice to him that said, "What are you doing here, Elijah?" (19:11–13)

And after Elijah had explained his fears, "the LORD said to him, 'Go, return on your way to the wilderness of Damascus'" (19:15a)—"I have a job for you to do there." How often we think, in order for it to be God's work, it must be spectacular, on the scale of windstorms and earthquakes and conflagrations! Our insurance policies even slander the one who loved creation into being by calling such destructive events "acts of God." But it was the still, small voice that God was in—not the rumbling thunder of digital "surround sound," but a silence so intense that Elijah could hear a whisper: "Go, continue on your journey. I have work for you to do."

Jesus came to the country of the Gerasenes and encountered there a man possessed with demons, naked, inhabiting the cemetery. He had been this way "for a long time" (Luke 8:26), Luke tells us. The residents of the place had become used to his condition, saw no reason to try to do anything about it, accepted it and accommodated themselves to it. Sometimes they would bind him in chains and shackles, but then he would once again work his way free and run into the wilderness, where still things didn't change— the man's torment, the man's indignity, the man's misery. Jesus found the man's plight intolerable. He sought to name the demons, the first step in curing the situation. They were "legion" (8:31)—a whole multitude, apparently, since a legion was five or six thousand soldiers.

Jesus called these many demons out of the man and cast them into a herd of pigs—of course, Jews shouldn't have had anything to do with swine to begin with—and the pigs all ran off headlong into the lake and drowned. The swineherds, deprived now of their livelihood, went out and told everyone they could find what Jesus had done, probably in the way of a complaint. "Then people came out to see what had happened, and when they came to Jesus, they found the man from whom the demons had gone sitting at the feet of Jesus, clothed and in his right mind" (8:35a–b). If *they* had been in *their* "right mind," if *they* had not been possessed of an unclean spirit, so to speak, they would have *rejoiced* that the man's *torment* was *over*, that his *dignity* had been *restored*, that he had been *saved*. But instead, "they were afraid" (8:35c), and "all the people of the surrounding country of the Gerasenes asked Jesus to leave them" (8:37a)—asked the one who was powerful enough and compassionate enough to cure a person of demons to be gone. How many people *today* witness the mighty acts of God, but, because they upset the way things are, perhaps even threaten entrenched economic interests and the appetites and expectations upon which they have planned their lives and made their investments and formed their opinions, would just as soon Jesus did his work of salvation somewhere else?

The experience of God's people is not primarily a matter of doctrine or law, but first and foremost a matter of activity and grace. It is a history of God taking the initiative to heal and liberate and restore—all of which is what the Bible means when it uses the word "save." And in so many of the stories about God's activity and grace, God used earthly instruments—people otherwise unremarkable, people often untrained, people pretty much like you and me, people pursuing their normal, daily lives of faithfulness to God. That history of salvation did not end with the last page of scripture; it continues today, in the very same ways that we read of in the Bible, sometimes in big events, more often in quiet and simple ways that will never be trumpeted in headlines or find their way into bestsellers, often the result of God's word of encouragement and challenge that come in moments of intense silence at the end of a disappointing, even frightening, day, often recognized only in retrospect. People of thin faith or occasional faith or no faith may find God's activity to be inconvenient, unpatriotic, or scandalous and might challenge the notion that it is God's activity at all—miracles only happen in the Bible, salvation has no claim upon my pocketbook, don't mix religion and politics. But God continues to work in real time, in the real situations that you and I encounter today in the home, in the school, in the workplace, in the church, in the halls of government, in the workings of nature, sometimes quietly, hardly noticeable. And the things that God is doing today are *still* the works of salvation.

Thirteenth Sunday in Ordinary Time
Spanish Springs Presbyterian Church, Sparks, Nevada
July 1, 2007

2 Kings 2:1–2, 6–14
Galatians 5:1, 13–25
Luke 9:51–62

"To Be a Disciple"

The life of a prophet was not an easy one. We saw last week how Elijah, who had shown the superiority of the God of Israel over the idol Baal and had brought about the massacre of Baal's prophets as God had commanded him, ended up a marked man. He was wanted dead or alive by Jezebel the queen of Israel, who was a worshiper of Baal. Terrified and discouraged, Elijah fled and hid in a cave. He *might* have expected to be hailed as a *hero*, if for no other reason than the end of the drought that followed the massacre of Baal's prophets. But his faithfulness to God had only gotten him into trouble with the authorities. He was a fugitive now, and anyone who *associated* with him would be in jeopardy, too. But, fulfilling a directive from God, as Elijah headed on to his next assignment, he had thrown his mantle over *Elisha*, who was to be his successor.

Elisha followed him but, after they left Gilgal, Elijah bade his protégé to remain behind while he himself went on to Bethel. "As the Lord lives, and you yourself live," said the younger man, "'I will not leave you'" (2 Kgs 2:2b). So they *both* went down to Bethel. Then, after they left Bethel, Elijah *again* bade his protégé to remain behind while he himself went on to Jericho. "As the Lord lives, and you yourself live," the younger man said again, "'I will not leave you'" (2:4b). So they *both* went down to Jericho. Then, after they left Jericho, Elijah *again* bade his protégé to remain behind while he himself went on to the Jordan. "As the Lord lives, and as you yourself live,'" the younger man said yet again, "'I will not leave you.' So the two of them went on. Fifty men of the company of prophets also went, and stood at some distance from them, as they both were standing by the Jordan. Then Elijah took his mantle and rolled it up, and struck the water; the water was parted to the one side and to the other, until the two of them crossed on dry ground. When they had crossed, Elijah said to Elisha, 'Tell me what I may do for you, before I am taken from you.' Elisha said, 'Please let me inherit a double share of your spirit'" (2:6b–9). Now, a "double share" doesn't mean that *Elisha* would be greater than *Elijah*. The "double share" means double the inheritance that anyone *else* would receive—the share of inheritance that would fall to a first-born son, along with the *responsibility* that would fall on a first-born son to carry on the family traditions and care for the family's welfare. Elijah responded to Elisha's request for such an inheritance and such a responsibility, "'You have asked a hard thing; yet, if you see me as I am being taken from you, it will be granted you; if not, it will not'" (2:10). Elijah, rightly, was leaving the granting of Elisha's request up to God.

> As they continued walking and talking, a chariot of fire and horses of fire separated the two of them, and Elijah ascended in a whirlwind into heaven. Elisha kept watching and crying out, "Father, father! The chariots of Israel and its horsemen!" But when [Elisha] could no longer see [Elijah], he grasped his own clothes and tore them in two pieces.
>
> He picked up the mantle of Elijah that had fallen from him, and went back and stood on the bank of the Jordan. He took the mantle of Elijah that had fallen from him, and struck the water, saying, "Where is the Lord, the God of Elijah?" When he had struck the water, the water was parted to the one side and to the other, and Elisha went over.
>
> When the company of prophets who were at Jericho saw him at a distance, they declared, "The spirit of Elijah rests on Elisha." They came to meet him and bowed to the ground before him. (2:11–15)

And after that, Elisha performed miracles that remind us of the miracles that *Elijah* had performed—an abundance of oil from a single jar, raising back to life again a mother's son who had died, and more, even.

Elijah knew from his own experience that being a spokesperson for God was not only *not easy*, it was *dangerous* and, humanly speaking, *thankless*. There would likely be temptation to doubt. There would likely be temptation to quit. There would likely be times when he wondered whether what he was doing was advancing God's agenda at all. But Elisha passed several tests for inheriting the prophetic office from Elijah. He demonstrated his loyalty to his master, he followed Elijah's circuitous journey without wavering, he gave the right answer to the test of making a final request of his master, and he walked *with* his master right up to the last moment. If any disciple was ever prepared to succeed his master in a difficult calling, it was Elisha. And, so, he was permitted to see the fiery chariot and its team and the ascent of Elijah into heaven. And Elisha became a great prophet, taunted and jeered sometimes, dreaded and reviled by some who were in power, but a faithful spokesperson for God.

Luke was well aware of these stories when he wrote about Jesus and the people around him—people who *were* his disciples and people who thought that they *wanted* to be his disciples. Luke was an associate of Paul, and Paul, as he knew, had suffered torture and imprisonment and, according to tradition, was executed for his faith by authorities in Rome. So, Luke was well aware of the costliness of being a follower of Christ. And, in his Gospel, he told of four incidents that illustrate that following Christ is a serious business, one for which, frankly, not everyone is suited. The disciples had gotten into an argument about which of them was the greatest; Jesus said that the greatest would be the one who was *least* among them, most like a little child, without claim, without privilege, without prestige. Then one of the disciples complained about a man, not one of their number, who was casting out demons; Jesus said that if the man was doing good works, he should be permitted to continue. Then, when some Samaritan villagers refused to receive Jesus, two of the disciples asked if they should have the village destroyed; Jesus rebuked them for even proposing such a thing.

In each of these three incidents, Jesus' followers showed that they were not really his disciples; they did not yet grasp what Jesus was about, and so they were not yet prepared to carry on his ministry. Disciples of Jesus must exhibit and be all about love, joy, peace, patience, kindness, generosity, faithfulness, gentleness, and self-control. As yet, the people traveling with Jesus were still jealous, angry, quarrelsome, factious, vengeful. They were interested in asserting themselves, in prohibiting, in getting even—things that would not do for a prophet, things that would not do for a servant of the Servant. Nor, the *next* episode shows, would delay or rationalization or self-promotion.

"As they were going along the road"—the road that Jesus was traveling to Jerusalem, and to the cross—"someone said to him, 'I will follow you wherever you go'" (Luke 9:57). *Many* of us would like to be such a person, perhaps believe that we *are*—offering ourselves whole-heartedly, so we think, to the Master. But it is easy to get caught up in the excitement of the moment. It may be that this person was impetuous by nature, easily carried away by emotions or by rhetoric or by dreams. Jesus quickly brought him down to earth, not, I think, being unkind, but honest. Was the man *really* prepared to be a *disciple*? "'Foxes have holes,'" Jesus said, "'and birds of the air have nests; but the Son of Man has nowhere to lay his head'" (9:58). Would this man be willing to face the rejection, even the persecution, even the martyrdom, that very likely awaited *anyone* who was walking the road that *Jesus* was walking? Jesus seems to have suspected that anyone who would offer him- or herself for such a life, and, possibly, death, did not perceive who Jesus was and what faithfulness to him would require.

"To another [Jesus] said, 'Follow me'" (9:59a). The Gospels suggest that it is more appropriate to *respond* to Jesus' *call* than to *force* oneself *upon* him. And if one acknowledges the authority of Jesus, that person will respond immediately and without qualification. "But [the man] said, 'Lord, first let me go and bury my father'" (9:59b). The call of Jesus is *always* urgent, and more urgent than any other business that is on our agenda—even the most pious duties imposed by religious law. The good religious people of that time, the good religious people of *any* time, would have considered properly burying one's parent to be among the highest moral obligations. Luke does not suggest here that the man was simply making up an *excuse* for not obeying Jesus and becoming his disciple. But, in the end, it amounted to the same thing. "Jesus said to him, 'Let the dead bury their own dead; but as for you, go and proclaim the kingdom of God'" (9:60). The physically dead are beyond the need of an evangelist, but it is vital that all who are still alive should hear the gospel.

"Another said, 'I will follow you, Lord; but let me first say farewell to those at my home'" (9:61). What could be more reasonable? Would Jesus want the man's family to wonder what had happened to him, that he simply disappeared, and without any parting word of affection? But, again, nothing must be more important for the disciple than following Jesus, now, immediately. When Jesus calls, there must be no competition for his lordship, not even the care of family, which, in some Christian circles, has nearly reached the status of idolatry. "Jesus said to him, 'No one who puts a hand to the plow and looks back is fit for the kingdom of God'" (9:62). You can't plow a straight furrow if your attention is on what's *behind* you, but only by setting your sight on what lies ahead, without distraction.

Luke reported these episodes not simply to let us know what happened once upon a time, but as an important message to anyone who was considering being Christ's disciple in the early days of the church, and to anyone who would consider being Christ's disciple today. This morning, we baptize five individuals, initiating them into the household of faith, washing them clean, submerging their old selves, and welcoming them to the new life that is theirs in Christ by the power of the Holy Spirit. What we do here marks them as Christ's own, his true disciples walking the road to the cross, which is the way to eternal life. It is clothing them with the garments of Christian love, but also with the mantle of Christian responsibility. They are freed from self-love to become, through love, slaves of one another, bearing a yoke of care for the world. May they, and all of us together, daily grow in our understanding of what it means to be Christ's disciples, and, day by day, more and more, become Christ's disciples indeed.

Fourteenth Sunday in Ordinary Time
First Presbyterian Church, Dodge City, Kansas
June 28, 1998

2 Kings 5:1–14
Galatians 6:1–16
Luke 10:1–11, 16–20

"So Much for Pride"

Looking forward to Independence Day, we should remember that, no matter how firmly convinced a people are that *their* nation is favored by God, God is *free* and may well *assert* that freedom to withdraw divine blessing or to bestow it upon some *other* people. The first sentence of our Old Testament reading from the Jewish scriptures is remarkable in its candor that it was *God* who had given victory to Israel's *enemy*. The *Arameans*, that is, the *Syrians*, had defeated *Israel* in battle. Apparently, they had even taken some Israelite captives as *slaves*. "Naaman, commander of the army of the king of Aram, was a great man," the Bible declares, "and [he was] in high favor with his master, because by *him* the Lord had given victory to *Aram*" (2 Kgs 5:1a). No doubt, Naaman the general returned to Damascus from the battlefield to a hero's welcome—streets lined with cheering citizens, waving tree branches and shouting slogans of praise. The king was well pleased. Whether Naaman or his king actually knew that *God* was behind the victory, the Bible doesn't say, but the author of the books of Kings certainly knew where the credit belonged.

But every life is a mixture of blessing and tragedy, and Naaman's was no exception. Great and heroic as he was, Naaman suffered from a skin disease, no doubt painful and unsightly. One day, his wife's slave girl, an *Israelite* lass who had compassion for her master, commented that there was a prophet in Samaria, the capital of Israel, who could cure Naaman. When

Naaman heard that someone had the ability to heal him of his leprosy, he reported it to his king. The king granted him permission to seek out the prophet and also said that he would notify the king of *Israel* that Naaman was coming to *his* territory to be *cured.*

The king of Israel undoubtedly remembered his *last* encounter with Naaman, the commander of the Aramean army, and the defeat that Israel had suffered at his hand. When Naaman then showed up on his doorstep with a letter that read, "I have sent to you my servant Naaman, that you may cure him of his leprosy" (5:6), the king of Israel, who had never cured *anybody* of *anything,* tore his clothes in distress. Regrettably, the king of Aram had not been any too precise in his message about just who it was he had been told could *perform* such a miracle. "Am I God, to give death or life, that this man sends word to me to cure a man of his leprosy? Just look and see how he is trying to pick a quarrel with me" (5:7). The king of Israel thought that it was all a provocation, a pretext, an excuse for another attack, for he would of course fail to do what the king of Aram knew was impossible for him to do—cure someone of leprosy.

Fortunately, he hadn't gotten down to his underwear yet when the prophet Elisha heard about it all and sent a message to the king of Israel. "Why have you torn your clothes? Let him come to *me,* that he may learn that there is a prophet in Israel" (5:8b). Of course, this is what the slave girl had meant all along—*Elisha* was the one she had told her mistress would be able to cure Naaman the leper. So Naaman went from the king's palace to Elisha's house, surely modest in comparison, and pulled up in front of the place with his whole entourage of chariots and horses and soldiers. Now, this is a comical thing—the great and mighty general who had defeated Israel's army had come down to Samaria with all of his horses and all of his men to see if Elisha could put him back together again—cure his leprosy—all lined up out in the street, just waiting for Elisha to come out and bow and be impressed. Can't you just see him there in his glistening military regalia sitting atop his handsome horse in the hot sun, and all his perspiring troops at attention, and no Elisha? Finally, someone in the household must have noticed the army parked out at the curb, and they hustled to Elisha's study and told him, and Elisha, busy at some other task, sent out a messenger to tell the great Naaman to go jump in the river seven times.

Naaman's response was predictable: "Doesn't he know who I am?—the great Naaman? Why doesn't he snap his fingers and command his God to cleanse me? I didn't have to come all the way to *Samaria* to go for a swim! I'll bathe in the *Syrian* rivers, thank you, if *that's* all he's going to do for me!" And scripture says, "He turned and went away in a rage" (5:12c).

Pride is perhaps the most dangerous of all emotions. In fact, scripture indicates that it's a *sin*, and it lies at the root of almost every *other* sin. It is *so harmful*, in fact, that it can even prevent a person from being healed of what ails him or her. In the Greek of the New Testament, the word for "heal" is the same as the word for "save." Pride can stand in the way of our *salvation* every bit as much as it can stand in the way of our being *cured*. If we can imagine a person too proud to take a bath in a muddy stream, or too proud to bare his or her behind for a hypodermic needle, or too proud to agree to a life-saving amputation, or too proud to ask for assistance in a public place when feeling dizzy or short of breath or sick to the stomach, perhaps we also can imagine a person being too proud to ask for forgiveness of someone he or she has wronged, or too proud to sell all of one's possessions and give the proceeds to the poor, or too proud to work in the homeless shelter, or too proud to kneel before God and say, "God, be merciful to me, a sinner!" (Luke 18:13b). We sacrifice so much for pride—sometimes, even our health, maybe even our salvation.

Fortunately for Naaman, he had servants who loved him. They approached him, still fuming over the perceived insult, and said to him, "'Father, if the prophet had commanded you to do something difficult, would you not have done it?'" (2 Kgs 5:13a). Wouldn't Naaman seek to the ends of the earth for some herb that the prophet had prescribed? Wouldn't he endure the pain of having the dead skin scraped off, if that were required? Wouldn't he swallow the most bitter medicine, if he thought it would cure him? "'How much more,'" the servant continued, "'when all he said to you was, "Wash, and be clean?"'" (5:13b). Naaman could not argue against the reasonableness of his servant, someone whose station in life meant that he was well practiced in humility. "So he went down and immersed himself seven times in the Jordan, according to the word of the man of God; his flesh was restored like the flesh of a young boy, and he was clean. Then he returned to [Elisha] the man of God, he and all his company; he came and stood before [Elisha] and said, 'Now I know that there is no God in all the earth except in Israel'" (5:14–15).

Sometimes, pride does damage to entire groups of people. Whole nations can be victims of their own pride. Look what the wounded pride of the German people after World War I resulted in. Think how our own nation's pride may have blinded us to the realities of Viet Nam. As a church historian, I have decided that it is *pride* as much as *theology* that has perpetuated many of the divisions within Christendom—Roman Catholic and Orthodox, for example, and Presbyterian and Lutheran, though both of these breaches are finally being addressed, if not quite repaired. The very notion of denominationalism, some of it starting with theological distinctions, much of it the result of ethnic background, some from linguistic differences, is always explained as a striving for doctrinal purity, but it is really evidence of human pride. And *Christ's glory* is *diminished* each time *our pride* claims its *pedestal*.

The cause of Christ has suffered so much for pride. The apostle Paul detected that pride was at the root of the rejection of *Gentile* believers by Christians of *Jewish* background. Writing to converts in the Greek regions of Galatia, Paul explained, "Even the circumcised do not themselves obey the law, but they want *you* to be circumcised so that *they* may *boast* about *your flesh*" (Gal 6:13). Paul himself saw only *one* appropriate basis for prideful boasting. "May I never boast of *anything* except the *cross of our Lord Jesus Christ*, by which the *world* has been crucified to *me*, and *I* to the *world*. For neither circumcision nor uncircumcision is anything; but a new creation is everything!" (6:14-15). The only proper response to our salvation in Jesus Christ is not *pride*, but *faith*—faith that replaces all need to *raise* ourselves, faith that replaces all need to *prove* ourselves, faith that replaces all need to *save* ourselves. Pride usurps the throne of Christ. Pride keeps us from serving others. Pride prevents us from seeking forgiveness. Pride stands in the way of our being healed of our sins.

From the very beginning, Jesus recognized that his followers would be tempted to unfaithfulness by human pride. It would seduce disciples from obedience. It would compromise their motives. When he sent seventy disciples out into hostile Samaritan territory, he told them to travel light and to live without complaint from whatever hospitality was offered them. "'Carry no purse, no bag, no sandals . . . . [E]at what is set before you; cure the sick . . . and say to them, "The kingdom of God has come near to you"'" (Luke 10:4a, 8b-9). When the seventy returned from their mission, joyful, they said, "'Lord, in your name even the demons submit to us!' He said to them, 'I watched Satan fall from heaven like a flash of lightning. See, I have given you authority to tread on snakes and scorpions, and over all the power of the enemy; and nothing will hurt you. Nevertheless, do not rejoice at this, that the spirits submit to you, but rejoice that your names are written in heaven'" (10:17b-20).

Not a few followers of Jesus have succumbed to the temptations of pride. That is why denominational in-fighting and battles within congregations become so fierce. Our beloved prejudices and our favorite doctrines and our pet projects have a tendency to become holier even than the crucified and risen Lord Jesus Christ. Ministers are susceptible, and not just television evangelists and the captains of the mega-churches. Like generals of old, in a few moments of a perceived affront, they can forget the very reason for faith's pilgrimage—to be made whole, cured of our diseases, saved from our sins, made strong and fit to serve God by serving humankind in the merciful and generous and humble manner of Jesus Christ, who willingly endured even the shame of the cross.

It is unlikely that anyone had ever treated Naaman with such insolence as Elisha did—sending a *messenger* out to tell him to go for a swim! What was this Elisha to him? The prophet of a subject people, whom he, Naaman, had defeated in battle and made a present of to the king of Aram!—who was Elisha to treat the war hero so casually? But Naaman was finally persuaded to do as Elisha said. And "his flesh was restored like the flesh of a young boy, and he was clean. Then he returned to the man of God, he and all his company; [Naaman] came and stood before [Elisha] and said, 'Now I know that there is no God in all the earth except in Israel; please accept a present from your *servant*'" (2 Kgs 5:14b–15). The great general had experienced salvation by the power of the only true God, and he now willingly accepted for himself the place and attitude of a slave. So much for pride.

Fifteenth Sunday in Ordinary Time

Amos 7:7–17
Colossians 1:1–14
Luke 10:25–37

"What God Commands"

"Which one of these three, do you think, was a neighbor to the man who fell into the hands of the robbers?" (Luke 10:36) Jesus asked the lawyer who had, Luke says, posed a question to Jesus in order to test him: "What must I do to inherit eternal life?" (10:25). Was it the *priest*, scrupulous to keep himself pure and holy by passing by the man lying in need on the other side of the road? Was it the *Levite*, a priestly assistant, who likewise was obliged not to come into contact with anything that might defile him and who, perhaps, didn't want to be inconvenienced by unpleasant contact with a man beaten and bloodied? Or was it the *Samaritan*, himself despised and avoided and criticized by proper Jewish society, who bandaged the man's wounds and took him to shelter and cared for him? "The one who showed him mercy," the lawyer replied, making the obvious choice when Jesus put the hypothetical before him so dramatically.

We know the story. And we know how Jesus turned the lawyer's question around from "Who is my neighbor?" to "Who was neighbor to the person in need?"—how the lawyer had asked Jesus what the limit of his compassion could be, and how Jesus instructed him that there *was* no limit so long as anyone was in need. Jesus' answer to the lawyer's question about inheriting eternal life had been simply to follow what the Bible said to do. And what is that? "You shall love the Lord your God with all your heart, and with all your soul, and with all your strength, and with all your mind; and your neighbor as yourself" (10:27). And, when the lawyer disingenuously asked the *next* question, Jesus told the famous parable that dismantles any objections of propriety, any arguments for self-preservation, any rationalizations against generosity. And, in the case of the priest and the Levite, avoiding contact with the victim alongside the road was not merely a matter of aesthetics or unpleasantness, but a matter of the ritual law—though the law well validated their sense of aesthetics and their desire to avoid unpleasantness.

Just so, a lot of churchgoers and even (or especially) ministers might feel relief of their sensibilities, perhaps even relief of their conscience, to learn that municipalities in various parts of our country have passed ordinances against giving money to beggars, have enacted laws against churches housing refugees. "You shall love the Lord your God with all your heart, and with all your soul, and with all your strength, and with all your mind; and your neighbor as yourself" (10:27). That's the law that we read in the Bible, clarified, as if it really needed any explanation, by Jesus' parable of the good Samaritan and Jesus' command, "Go and do likewise" (10:37). And councils and legislatures throughout history have responded with, "Thou shalt not do what Jesus commands."

The business of life, as the Bible boils it down, is to love God and to love others, and makes it clear that you can't love God if you don't love neighbors, and that loving neighbors means loving anyone who is in any way in need. There are a lot of specific commandments in the Bible, of course—and not just ten—but they all stem from or involve instances of the twin commands to love God and neighbor, found in Deuteronomy 6 and Leviticus 19 and elaborated by the whole rest of the Bible. And any earthly power that asserts authority to contradict the law of God claims to be superior to God. And it is the obligation of those who are loyal to God, who claim allegiance to God, who place obedience to God above every other responsibility, to resist that usurpation of God's primacy. Otherwise, believers in God, followers of God, in fact are not.

The contest between heavenly and earthly authority is as old as scripture, and "politics," broadly defined, is very much a subject of the Bible, because so much of history is about earthly attempts to trespass upon divine purpose and contradict divine command. Age-old calls to keep politics out of the church flatly ignore huge chunks of scripture and major concerns of the gospel. While partisanship, in the sense of championing one political party over another, is wisely prohibited in the American church, championing the causes of protecting and elevating the poor and the powerless and the friendless, the alien and the immigrant and the hungry, the sick and the homeless and the oppressed, and caring for individuals who are any of these, is being the neighbor that Jesus commands us to be. "Go and do likewise" (10:37). And woe be it to any Christian or any group of Christians who seeks to restrict the definition of the neighbor for whom we are to care

"What God Commands"   43

and whom we are to serve. And woe be it to any ruler who attempts to say that we may not, in fact, be a neighbor as Jesus commands, and woe be it to any government that by intention or neglect causes or allows anyone to go hungry or sick or homeless or oppressed, citizen or no, white Anglo Christian or no.

In the years after the northern tribes of Israel split away from the southern tribes of Judah, in the days of King Jeroboam II of Israel—the Northern Kingdom—God called upon a man from the Southern Kingdom of Judah, Amos, a herdsman and a tender of sycamore trees, to go prophesy in the Northern Kingdom and to declare God's judgment against Israel and the king. By that time, prophets were usually part of a guild, a school, an approved and officially recognized, traditionally trained corps of advisers to the king or to the priests, dependent, in fact, upon the established institutions of the nation and therefore disinclined and unlikely to constitute much of a threat to how things were and always had been. They were expected to soothe and comfort in tough times, not suggest that society's hardships were a result of God's displeasure or the simple consequences of ignoring God's wisdom. But Amos had been called to be a prophet directly by God, without the customary training and without official approval, and to deliver God's uncomfortable commands and harsh rebuke. It was because Israel had mistreated the poor, had exchanged truth for lies, had committed lust and incest, had corrupted and bribed the clergy and commanded God's prophets, "You shall not prophesy" (Amos 2:12b), that God had now vowed punishment and sent Amos to deliver the unwelcome judgment. Israel's occasional religious festivals were no delight to God when their entire culture had yielded to greed and pleasure and had made sure that the "haves" continued to have and the "have-nots" continued to have nothing. So, God had commanded this prophet, Amos, to prophesy and protest despite all the prohibitions against criticism of Israel, its king and his government and his claims over the priesthood and the official court and sanctuary prophets who were now nothing but sycophants, yes-men, cheerleaders for whatever the king wanted to do.

God had relented on previous occasions, had in fact turned away from the destruction of Israel that he had vowed when Amos had pleaded with him, "O Lord GOD, forgive, I beg you!" (7:2); "O Lord GOD, cease, I beg you!" (7:5). But finally, God had had enough. Divine forbearance had come to an end. God would allow Israel's destruction.

> This is what he showed me: the Lord was standing beside a wall built with a plumb line, with a plumb line in his hand.

The word usually translated as "plumb line" might actually mean "tin," referring to the metal used as an alloy in forging weapons, in fashioning swords.

> And the LORD said to me, "Amos, what do you see?" And I said, "A plumb line."

Again, the word most likely refers to a sword. Either way, the image is ominous and damning against Israel.

> Then the Lord said,
>> "See, I am setting a plumb line
>>> in the midst of my people Israel;
>>> I will never again pass them by;"—

I will never again indulge their disobedience, will never again relent from punishing their sinfulness—

> "the high places of Isaac shall be made desolate,
>> and the sanctuaries of Israel shall be laid waste,
>> and I will rise against the house of Jeroboam with the sword."
>> (7:7–9)

Frankly, folks, you and I should be trembling for fear of God's punishment when we pass by homeless encampments on our city's sidewalks, when we witness huddled masses behind the razor wire on our borders, when we nightly see on the news the dead and starving and wounded and homeless in Gaza and all the other war zones of the world. Is our society, is our culture, is our nation exempt from the command to love God with all our heart, soul, and strength, and to love our neighbor as ourselves? Are we smugly confident that there will be no penalty for ignoring or denying the Bible's most basic commandment? Will we decide it is better to shut up the prophets, perhaps criticize them for not being "pastoral," than to be bothered by the inconvenience of taking responsibility for and confronting and responding to the ills of our age, from poverty to racism to global environmental catastrophe? Amos was a marked man. Amaziah, the priest of Bethel, the official sanctuary of Israel's king not far from Israel's capital of Samaria, had reported to Jeroboam,

> "Thus Amos has said,
>> 'Jeroboam shall die by the sword,
>>> and Israel must go into exile
>>> away from this land.'"

> And Amaziah [the priest] said to Amos, "O seer, go, flee away to the land of Judah, earn your bread *there*, and prophesy *there*; but

never again prophesy at Bethel, for it is the *king's* sanctuary, and
it is a temple of the kingdom." (7:10–13)

Better that God's true prophet should be exiled than that the nation should hear that *it* was surely going to face exile for its disregard of the poor and the alien and the unlovely, as it in fact did when it was conquered by Assyria and its leaders were hauled away to be dispersed among the Gentiles and Gentiles were intermingled among its population, eventually setting the stage for Jews of Jesus' time to despise these "Samaritans," one of whom was the hero of Jesus' parable when he put God's law of compassion and hospitality above the rules of ritual purity that were so congenial to the priest's and Levite's attitudes of exclusion and disgust.

And Amos answered Amaziah,

> "The LORD took me from following the flock, and the LORD said to me,
> 'Go, prophesy to my people Israel.'
> "Now therefore hear the word of the LORD.
> You say, 'Do not prophesy against Israel,
>   and do not preach against the house of Isaac.'
> Therefore thus says the LORD:
> 'Your wife shall become a prostitute in the city,
>   and your sons and your daughters shall fall by the sword,
>   and your land shall be parceled out by line,
> you yourself shall die in an unclean land,
>   and Israel shall surely go into exile away from its land.'"
> (7:15–17)

So much for not mixing religion and politics. So much for religion being all about comfort and consolation. So much for the preacher being just a dispenser of cheap grace.

Nations still try to muzzle the prophets sent by God to declare the truth of what God wants and expects and how societies will suffer when they ignore or deny that truth. It was proverbial in ancient Judah that Jerusalem had a habit of stoning the prophets. The Bible doesn't actually tell us of any executions of the Old Testament prophets by stoning, but whether figuratively or literally, though unrecorded, the persistence of the saying must indicate that Israel's rulers and their sycophants who enjoyed the way things were must regularly have tried to silence God's messengers when their words became uncomfortable or inconvenient. And, in the New Testament, think of John the baptizer. Think of Jesus himself. And, among Jesus' followers, think of Stephen, and, later, according to reliable legend, Peter and Paul. And think of modern martyrs—Bonhoeffer, King, Romero. And all those who, while not murdered, have been ridiculed, jailed, defamed for daring to speak truth to power, daring even to challenge our own comforts and our own amusements and our own prejudices and our own lies.

There have always been those who thought that religion, even Judaism, even Christianity, exists to preserve the order that is and persuade its victims to silent endurance, deferring until some heavenly by-and-by the way that scripture says God wants things to be, blessing rather than judging the deeds of rulers and the habits of the privileged rather than condemning them and championing the powerless rather than rationalizing society's disregard and abuse. How many instances have there been in history of coopting the church, the religious establishment, to keep things the way they are despite the Bible's loud condemnation of entrenched and even institutionalized sin, and God's vow to punish it? "Unpatriotic!" "Treason!" And, perhaps most conclusively damning of all: "Impractical!" That is what is most problematic about displaying national flags in Christian sanctuaries—even more problematic than suggesting that God favors one nation over others or excuses its sins—that the church exists at the pleasure of, exists by the grace of, exists to serve, enjoys the approval and receives the favor of, the government and the culture it rules. Consider how the Nazi regime coopted and made the German church a department of the state, so that it spewed its venomous and hateful propaganda from the pulpit, so that it emasculated the gospel by transforming the Christ of God into a mascot of white Aryan nationalist imperialism and became a willing partner in the stigmatization and detention and even death of millions of Jews and gays and Romi and intellectuals, wrapping its cross in the swastika. It became a badge of political righteousness to pass by the bruised and bloodied victim of brutal and uncaring inhumanity lying on the side of the road. And, undoubtedly, the pulpit came to be popularly regarded as a place where the ruling order would be legitimized and praised and the role of the clergy was nothing at all like the preachers of olden days, those whom the Bible calls "prophets." But, ultimately, devastation will fall on any and all nations, societies, cultures that ignore or deny or simply neglect the commandment to love God with all one's heart and soul and strength and one's neighbor as oneself, and upon the religious institutions that prop up the structures that condone violence and oppression, inhumanity and the destructive ways of pride and self-indulgence, and mistreat the earth that God loves, and devalue any of the creatures for whom God cares passionately. And those who seek to silence God's prophets whom God has called and who therefore are compelled to declare the truth even when unpopular, even when uncomfortable, even when inconvenient, are guilty of contradicting God's command.

But we—we have been baptized into Christ Jesus. God has claimed us. We have been marked as Christ's own forever. Our standard, our plumb line, is the cross. Our citizenship, our loyalty, our allegiance, is first and foremost and all about God and God's command to love. "He has rescued us from the power of darkness and transferred us into the kingdom of his beloved Son," the Bible declares, "in whom we have redemption, the forgiveness of sins" (Col 1:13–14). And God's forgiveness makes repentance possible—turning away from the pride and self-indulgence, away from the false assurance and easy rationalization, and turning toward God and our neighbor. "But wanting to justify himself, [the lawyer] asked Jesus, 'And who is my neighbor?'" (Luke 10:29).

Sixteenth Sunday in Ordinary Time

Spanish Springs Presbyterian Church, Sparks, Nevada

July 18, 2010

Amos 8:1–12
Colossians 1:15–28
Luke 10:38–42

"Upsetting the Basket"

Of all God's complaints about the people of Israel recorded in the Bible, of all God's proclamations of judgment upon the people's unfaithfulness, there is none so utterly devoid of hope as the passage from the prophet Amos that we heard in this morning's Old Testament reading. Amos's words must have come as quite a shock to most people who heard them way back in the eighth century BC. They were not only unwelcome but virtually incomprehensible. Amos spoke them during the long and peaceful reign of King Jeroboam II, when the Northern Kingdom of Israel was at the height of its worldly success. The Northern Kingdom had expanded its borders to what would be the greatest territorial extent Israel would ever know. The nation's prosperity was unprecedented and would never be greater. And, rather naturally, the people interpreted their strong military security and great economic affluence as signs of God's favor and approval. No doubt, they thought, it had something to do with the fact that the people brought lavish gifts to the various shrines erected to the Lord—offerings that God must have found acceptable, homage for which God reciprocated with the gift of real estate and a huge GDP.

And then, here came this shepherd from Judea—Israel's rival and cousin to the south—who seems to have been history's greatest party pooper. He claimed that God had authorized him to denounce Israel's trust in her military might (and Judah's too, for that matter), and her social inequalities and injustices, and her empty piety at the altar. One of the prophet's most influential critics was Amaziah, the priest at Bethel, who told him to go home and "zip it" and never again darken the door of the shrine, to which Amos answered, in last Sunday's Old Testament reading, that Amaziah's wife would become a prostitute and Amaziah's children would all die violently and Amaziah's land would be taken from him and that Amaziah himself, the priest of God, would die among Gentiles—an insulting prophecy of mortifying proportions. And then God showed Amos a vision of a basket of summer produce, figs and olives and the like, signifying the end of the fruitful season in Israel's history—the Hebrew words for "summer fruit" and "end" sound much alike.

Then the LORD said to [Amos],

"The end has come upon my people Israel;
  I will never again pass them by.
The songs of the temple shall become wailings in that day," says the
  Lord GOD;
"the dead bodies shall be many,
  cast out in every place. Be silent!" (Amos 8:2b–3)

In all the Bible, there is no word of God so bleak as this. The people of Israel were about to be utterly cut off—the word translated as "end" is used other places in the scriptures to mean an "end of life." The Lord's pledge never again to pass by his people evidently means that there would be no more forgiveness. God had shown mercy for the last time. They had often been warned, from time to time they had even been punished, but still they persisted in their disobedient ways. There was nothing left to do but cut them off—and, in fact, shortly after Jeroboam's reign, Israel fell to the Assyrian Empire and never recovered, was never again an independent people, was always thereafter viewed with disdain by the Southern Kingdom, which itself was destined to fall to the Babylonians, but, unlike Israel, Judah would rise again to nationhood. By the time of Jesus, the people of Judah heaped scorn upon their northern neighbor, whom they considered to be heretical and unclean, the result of religious and ethnic impurity, and, as the Gospels reflect, they had nothing but contempt for the Samaritans—the people named after their old capital city, Samaria.

And what was the reason that God finally gave up on the northern tribes, finally turned his back on so many of Abraham's descendants, finally abandoned Israel to the swords and spears of the Gentiles from Assyria—she who *had* seemed so *charmed* among the nations?

Hear this, you that trample on the needy,

> and bring to ruin the poor of the land,
> saying, "When will the new moon be over
> so that we may sell grain;
> and the sabbath,
> so that we may offer wheat for sale?
> We will make the ephah small and the shekel great"—

meaning they would cheat their customers by selling an undersized amount and overcharging for it—

> "and practice deceit with false balances,
> buying the poor for silver
> and the needy for a pair of sandals,
> and selling the sweepings of the wheat" (8:4–6)—

selling grain to the poor by the pound but mixing in plenty of worthless chaff as filler.

Those of us who are in the Sunday morning class that is based on Marva Dawn's book about the sabbath[1] have been reminded that the seventh day is the goal of the six other days of the week, not the other way around. We live toward and work for the sabbath, on which there should be no striving or work. Sabbath is a gift from God that should fill us with anticipation and joyful longing for the *final* sabbath, when all will be at rest and we will spend eternity in worship and enjoyment of God. The sabbath is a judgment upon unrestrained money-making and preoccupation with personal security and the futility of trying to make one's own future. Amos proclaimed God's judgment that the people of Israel *observed* the sabbath all right, closing their shops and carting offerings to the shrine, but what good was it when all the time they were just chomping at the bit to get back to making money during the work week? (And in case you missed the relevance, this was the ancient equivalent of taking the briefcase and laptop and cell phone home with you for the weekend.) And not only *that*, but the way they were *making* money was to the detriment of the poor, selling polluted produce, using false weights and measures in the market, forcing people to sell themselves into slavery to pay their debts.

"Surely I will never forget any of their deeds" (8:7b), God declared. And here is a great difference between Amos and the other prophets—always, elsewhere, what God pledges *never to forget* is his covenant promise. God declares in many *other* passages that he *will* forget the people's wrongdoing. But, now, in Israel, the rich have trampled the poor one too many times. The sabbath has been turned upside down once too often. And, so, the basket is

---

1. Dawn, *Keeping the Sabbath Wholly.*

about to be upset. God's patience has come to an end. The promise not to forget is for the first time a *threat*, not a *consolation*. The people will perish. Their prosperous society, constructed on the backs of the poor and at the expense of fairness, and their national security, measured by soldiers and weapons rather than justice and generosity, are illusions that pervert their sabbath observance and make hypocritical their offerings to God. The ax is going to fall, and nothing will prevent it. A famine is coming worse than any famine of bread or thirst for water—the utter silence of God. And there will be no word of blessing or comfort from the Lord and his prophets, no encouragement about the future, no promise of forgiveness. Because of the way they have been treating each other, and despite their parades of piety, God has finally had it. What is the point of continuing to speak to the people when they don't listen? Everything has been said, but nothing ever changes, or only gets worse. Darkness is going to fall on Israel like a curtain right in the middle of the day, and the joyful feasts will become funerals, and the songs of praise will become dirges of grief. And all will be utter hopelessness, as if death had claimed one's only child. And the worst thing of all will be that God will walk out the door and close it behind him. While the people have been congratulating themselves on their strong economy and secure borders and interpreting it all as cornucopia, God has been counting their accomplishments as a measure of their faithlessness and disobedience. The basket of summer fruit, abundant and delectable, is about to be upset, exposing a profound emptiness where all had assumed a well-earned bounty. Israel is about to fall, not because of enemies from outside but from the social decay within, and Israel will not be able to get up again.

There are some who fault the Presbyterian Church and other mainline denominations for refusing to confine their teachings to "spiritual" matters, for spending resources and energy on concerns other than "salvation." One of the leading diagnoses of the decline of membership in the mainline churches is that they spend so much time and effort on social issues rather than, as the criticism goes, tending to the matter of people's souls. They should just limit themselves to the Bible and its concerns. And, besides that, people obviously aren't going to be attracted by preaching that seems like criticism of their way of life or the way they practice their livelihoods or anything that might smack of economics or politics. That's not going to draw anybody to the church. All this talk about the poor and the oppressed—how about some congratulations for those who pay the bills? All this judgment and lament stuff—don't people come to church in order to feel good about themselves? All this talk about greed and poverty and hunger and war and injustice—what does that have to do with my getting into heaven or not? What does that have to do with the Ten Commandments—with idolatry, with killing, with stealing, with honoring the elderly, with coveting, with slander, with sabbath?

> I will turn your feasts into mourning,
> and all your songs into lamentation" (8:10a)—

the *judgment* is going to *begin* at the house of the Lord! The church had jolly well be concerned about reforming Wall Street and banks and credit cards! No, it's not a matter that must be left to market forces. The church had better be talking about things like sharing wealth so that the hungry are fed and the homeless are housed and changing priorities so that the seas are cleaned up and the guns are laid down! No, it's not a matter that should be left to charity. God wasn't condemning Israel's lack of *charity*. God was condemning the greed and injustice and disregard of others' needs and others' lives that make charity *necessary*. God's mercy is boundless but God's patience is not, and the more laws there are that favor the *haves* over the have-*nots*, and the more society tempts itself to value *things* above *people*, and the more the culture excuses dishonesty and exploitation by bowing to the idols of stock values and profit margins, the nearer the time when God will judge our economic affluence and our political influence and will give up and close the door behind him. And we will be left thinking that the *basket* looked so *full* that it blinded us to the fact that so many *plates* were *empty*.

Doesn't that mean that the church must be involved in social issues? Doesn't that require that Christians regard the sabbath as something other than a quaint antique that has no place in today's amusement-craving, freedom-asserting, consumerist-oriented culture? Doesn't that oblige the church to give strong witness to God's repeated call for justice for the poor and the hungry and the powerless and the oppressed, to take so to heart the values of God that we should be practicing them each sabbath and living them out the rest of the week, celebrating them in worship and enacting them in our lives outside the sanctuary, not only bringing an offering to God on Sunday but sharing our blessings Monday through Saturday with those who are easily abused or exploited or simply forgotten in the world's rush to fortune and fame? How can anyone read the Gospels and not perceive that Jesus was always prompting people to consider whether their worship of God is genuine, whether their offerings are pleasing to the Father, whether their songs of praise are welcome in heaven? Looking at the basket of summer fruit, the self-secure and affluent society warmly congratulates itself for so obviously having won God's favor by means of its work and its wits. But the faithful and prophetic church will call society, and will challenge itself, to live in accordance with the words of God, lest we all wake up one day and find that God has abandoned us to the very godlessness that has ruled our marketplace and compromised our courthouse. What a terrible image:

> They shall wander from sea to sea,
>   and from north to east;
> they shall run to and fro, seeking the word of the LORD,
>   but they shall not find it. (8:12)

That's not what people *want* to hear. But it's something that people *need* to hear.

Last Tuesday afternoon, while in Alabama for the Hymn Society meeting at Samford University, I toured the Birmingham Civil Rights Institute Museum, just across the street from the 16th Street Baptist Church, where four girls were killed by a bomb blast while attending Sunday school, and also across the street from the park where marches were organized by Dr. King and others. The museum's exhibits are arranged in chronological order, from the founding of Birmingham in 1871 up to the time of the election of its first African-American mayor in the late 1970s. At one point, in the section where the story of the civil rights struggle in the 1960s is being told, I noticed a photograph of a group of men taking part in a march or demonstration and, in the middle of the group, a white man wearing a clerical collar. Underneath the picture were the names of the men, and the sole white minister in the group was identified as "Rev. Blake." Well, I knew the face—it was Eugene Carson Blake, the stated clerk of the General Assembly of the Presbyterian Church in the 1960s and president of the National Council of the Churches of Christ in the USA.

I am grateful to be part of a denomination, part of a tradition, that has been willing to upset some baskets now and then in order to draw attention to the will of God, hopeful that this isn't the day God will give up and walk away. "This is what the Lord GOD showed me—a basket of summer fruit. He said, 'Amos, what do you see?'" (8:1–2a).

Seventeenth Sunday in Ordinary Time
Spanish Springs Presbyterian Church, Sparks, Nevada
July 29, 2001

Hosea 1:2–10
Colossians 2:6–15
Luke 11:1–13

"The Anguish of God"

Our Presbyterian *Book of Order* contains very few "shall's" or "must's" when it comes to the order of worship. Frankly, some Presbyterian ministers ignore the strong advice in the *Book of Order* that commends the reading of scripture in public worship on the Lord's Day always including passages from the *Old* Testament—the Hebrew scriptures—as well as from the *New* Testament. The reason is so that the people of God *today* may hear the fullness of the story of God's work among the people of God in the *past*, the fullness of God's promise to the people of God *in all ages*, the *full* content of the hope that is ours *right now* in the life, death, and resurrection of Jesus Christ, to whom *all* of scripture points, not *just* the New Testament. The God who most perfectly revealed himself in Jesus Christ is the God who formed a people of whom we are the contemporary spiritual offspring, and we can neither understand Jesus Christ nor the faith in him that the Holy Spirit nurtures in us without hearing the witness of the Old Testament history, law, wisdom, psalms, and prophets.

    One of the characteristics of Old Testament prophecy is its insight into the *nature* of God. Recurring among nearly all the prophetical books is the testimony later enfleshed in Jesus Christ that God is not an aloof figure whose mind, once made up eons before the world was created, remains closed to changing. I have noticed, in my ministry, that the thought of God actually changing his mind might offend some people's orthodox notions of the all-knowing majesty of God, but it posed no difficulties at all for the prophets whom God called to declare the divine will to God's people. The God of the prophets is a God who *interacts* with creation. According to the Bible, God *responds* to situations and *adapts* to situations. Repeatedly in scripture, God even responds to human requests and appeals by *changing his mind*. While we may have trouble confessing that in our *creeds*, in practice we *depend* upon it in our prayer life. For one important result of God's ability and willingness to change his mind is that, as Jesus declares in our Gospel text this morning, God can be counted on to answer prayers. It *also* means that, in some sense that is surely different from human experience, and yet not totally different, God has *feelings*, God has *passions*.

Some of us may picture God as someone who once wound up the universe like a clock and then went on about some other business, while the world runs *on* or runs *down* without any further attention from its creator. But that is not the God of the prophets. The prophets speak of a God who is in *relationship* with creation, or *wants* to be, and being in *relationship* renders God emotionally *vulnerable*. The great designer and sustainer of the universe is sensitive enough to be *bewildered* when his love is not *returned*. The God who called a nation into being and brought it up out of slavery by holding back the tides is susceptible to sorrowful anger when his gracious favor is met with callous indifference, and when his people are not gracious or are indifferent toward one another. The God who stretched the heavens and raised the mountains and filled the seas is not so much a judge who must safeguard his honor by punishing us when we break a law, but a heavenly parent who cries in bed at night worrying about a wayward child, a steadfast friend who cannot abide to live in the loneliness of a friendship that has gone sour, an eternal lover whose heart is broken by the liaisons of a faithless spouse.

Do we have trouble thinking of God in these terms? Perhaps we should consider whether we have allowed our doctrines to outrun the scriptures, or whether we have been reading the Bible through some thick preconceptions. And, just maybe, it means that we should reconsider what sort of relationship God wants with us and whether we are doing enough to promote peace in the world and justice in society and generosity toward the foreigner, the poor, and the oppressed—all things that the prophets proclaimed as God's special interests.

The image of marriage as the relationship between God and God's chosen people appears in several places in the Old and New Testaments, but nowhere more poignantly than in the book of Hosea. Hosea was the prophet whom God directed to go and take for himself "a wife of whoredom" and "to have children of whoredom." "For," as God said to Hosea, "the land commits great whoredom by forsaking the LORD" (Hos 1:2). So, Hosea went and took Gomer, and she bore him a son. The Lord instructed Hosea to name the boy "Jezreel." God said that he would soon punish the royal house for the massacre it committed at the town of Jezreel when it usurped the monarchy, and that the valley of Jezreel would be the scene of a tremendous defeat of Israel's army by the Assyrians. Then Gomer conceived and bore a daughter, and God told Hosea to call the girl "Not Pitied," for God would no longer have pity on the house of Israel and would no longer forgive its wrongs. Then Gomer conceived and bore another son, whom the Lord directed Hosea to name "Not my people," for in the sense that they had broken the covenant God made with Moses—"I will take you as my people, and I will be your God" (Exod 6:7a)—Israel was no longer the people of God and the God of the covenant was no longer the God of Israel. And Hosea had a turbulent marriage, Gomer going out and bedding down with other men, just as Israel had turned its back on the ways of God and upon God's special concern for the poor and the refugee and the dispossessed. But God directed Hosea to go out and find his errant wife and bring her home again.

The message that the prophet Hosea was to deliver was woven into the fabric of his own life. The painful marriage to a prostitute was not a way for God to speak to Hosea, but a way for God to speak *through* Hosea to *Israel*. The prophet's own children, by their very names, were reminders, every time roll was called in school or sides were chosen at recess for a baseball game, that Israel had been unfaithful and had cut itself off from the mercy of God. But there would also be a future when the covenant would be *renewed*—when God would *honor* the ancient promise to Abraham by *increasing* the number of his descendants, and the decimation of God's judgment would be eclipsed by the bounty of God's salvation. Hosea's life was a parable of God's *frustration* but also of God's redeeming and steadfast *love*.

You can perhaps imagine how painful it was for me during seminary to receive notice, shortly after my first wife left our home and started living with another man, that my Old Testament exam for ordination would be on the book of Hosea. We were not given the verses for the examination beforehand, just the fact that it would be a passage selected from Hosea. Naturally, I began reading everything I could on Hosea, cataloguing in my mind the themes of the book and the circumstances under which it was written, so far as we know them, and doing word studies on some of the key terms. The pain, the grief, the anger, the bewilderment, and the loneliness of abandonment and betrayal were all fresh. The wounds of my heart were still bleeding freely. I do not think that God intended *my* situation to be a public pronouncement, but I had some new insight, as Hosea himself had once gained, into the pain, the grief, the anger, the bewilderment, and the

"The Anguish of God"

loneliness of God. Was my sense of justice offended? Absolutely, and utterly. But my hurt was much more than an offended sense of justice; it was *anguish* deep, deep in my heart. And that is the *sort* of anguish, the book of Hosea makes clear to us, that *God* feels when we who have pledged to love him run after *other* gods, and seek *other* standards by which to live our lives and on which to order our society, everything from nursing private grudges to not caring that someone is denied a job because of the color of their skin or the language that they speak or the gender with which they were born, everything from careless speech that curses or slanders to deeds that intentionally demean and destroy—all of these wrench the heart of God with an anguish that is like the unfaithfulness of a spouse.

Half a century ago, the Jewish biblical scholar Abraham Heschel observed,

> The bricks we collect in order to construct the biblical image of God are, as a rule, conceptual notions, such as goodness, justice, wisdom, unity. [But] in terms of *frequency* of usage in biblical language, they are *surpassed* by statements referring to God's *pathos*....
>
> To the prophet . . . God does not reveal himself in an abstract absoluteness, but in a personal and intimate relation to the world. [God] does not simply command and expect obedience. [God] is also moved and affected by what *happens* in the world, and reacts accordingly. Events and human actions arouse in [God] joy or sorrow, pleasure or wrath. [God] is not conceived as judging the world in detachment. [God] reacts in an intimate and subjective manner, and thus determines the value of events. Quite obviously in the biblical view [wrote Heschel], [human] deeds may move Him, affect Him, grieve Him or, on the other hand, gladden and please Him....
>
> [God] is personally *involved* in, even *stirred* by, the conduct and fate of [humankind].[1]

God, in other words, is a God who can and does suffer, a God who experiences anguish at human faithlessness, ingratitude, and rebellion.

The decisions that we make, the deeds that we do, the words that we speak do not simply have the potential of violating some impersonal law that God dictated once upon a time to show that he is the boss of the universe; they have a real effect upon the feelings of God today. They affect God deeply, and they affect our *relationship* with God. Human sin affects not only the *sinner*; it sullies God's beloved creation for which God has labored

---

1. Heschel, *Prophets, Part II*, 2, 3–4. Emphasis added.

eons. "Then the LORD said [to Hosea when the third child was born], 'Name him Lo-ammi ["Not my people"], for you are not my people and I am not your God'" (Hos 1:9). The special relationship established long years before in the wilderness between God and Moses, that had given promise of fulfilling God's purpose for creation, had come to an end. The people had gone after *other* gods called Baal—the fertility gods of Canaan, doing the things that the world said would ensure good crops or, to contemporize a bit, doing the things that would maximize profits and provide security regardless of the effects upon others of God's creatures and regardless that it implied a distrust of God's promises to provide all that we need. "[Israel] did not know," said the Lord,

> that it was *I* who gave her
> the grain, the wine, and the oil,
> and who lavished upon her silver
> and gold that *they* used for [casting *idols*]. (2:8)

Can you hear the *anguish* in those words of God who created the world and peopled it out of love, so that there might be creatures to have friendship with and to care for, and so overcome the otherwise indescribable loneliness of being God? Alienation is not God's *choice*. God is sorrowfully dismayed by the incredible human unfaithfulness by which we alienate ourselves from him. The situation is not just a matter of breaking God's laws, but of breaking God's heart: "For you are not my people and I am not your God" (1:9b). When we follow yearnings of pride and selfishness and greed and prejudice, God reacts not by reckoning it on some eternal ledger sheet, but by sitting up all night with a light in the window, anxious that we will come home without having done too much harm to ourselves or to others.

The *good news* is that, despite all the pain of a spouse forsaken and betrayed, there is one thing about which God does *not* change his mind: God's ultimate purpose is the salvation of the loving relationship which is the foundation of creation. Repeatedly, God has had every reason to say, as he does in the book of Hosea,

> Woe to them, for they have strayed from me!
> Destruction to them, for they have rebelled against me! (7:13a–b)

But God's compassion born of his faithfulness to us and to himself always *restrains* the divine anger, though it be ever so justified.

> I will *heal* their disloyalty;
> I will love them freely,
> for my anger has turned from them. (14:4)

> On that day, says the LORD, you will call me, "My husband".... I will make for you a covenant on that day with the wild animals, the birds of the air, and the creeping things of the ground; and I will abolish the bow, the sword, and war from the land; and I will make you lie down in safety. And I will take you for my wife forever, I will take you for my wife in righteousness and in justice, in steadfast love, and in mercy. I will take you for my wife in faithfulness; and you shall know the LORD. (2:16a, 18-20)

There are people in this sanctuary who have been through the same sort of thing that I once endured. We know that, for a long time, no matter how hurt and humiliated we were by our spouse's unfaithfulness, we wanted more than anything to have that person back. Eventually, the impossibility of that becomes clear, and maybe even the *imprudence* of that becomes clear, and love fades. The anguished yearning wanes—rightly and *healthily*, we say from a *psychological* point of view, enabling us to get on with our lives rather than pining over a hopeless situation. But *God's* hope is never extinguished, even as God's anguish is never exhausted, because God's love, in its perfection, never ends. How can any of us bear the thought of causing anguish to a God who is so compassionate, so merciful, so gracious, so generous, so sensitive, so vulnerable, so loving?

Eighteenth Sunday in Ordinary Time
Spanish Springs Presbyterian Church, Sparks, Nevada
August 5, 2001

Hosea 11:1–11
Colossians 3:1–11
Luke 12:13–21

"Focus on a Far Horizon"

In Alistair MacLeod's recent novel, *No Great Mischief*, Alexander MacDonald, the character who narrates the story, a native of Nova Scotia's Cape Breton, tells of attending an orthodontists' convention in Dallas. Another conventioneer noticed his nametag, at a cocktail party or some such event, and started quizzing him about all the Ukrainians who had settled in Canada, and weren't they really Russians?

"They're people from the Ukraine," [Alexander responded]. "That's where they're from."

"No" he said. "There's no such place. They're Russians. I looked it up on the map."

"No, they're not Russians. The map changes."

"When I look at a map," he said, "I believe those lines. I believe it like I believe an X-ray . . . There aren't any Ukrainians. They're Russians'"

"It's not that simple," I said pointlessly again.

"I hear the Communists are taking over the medical system in Canada," he said. "That's why I asked the question."

"No," I said. "That's not that simple either."

"You keep saying everything's not that simple," he said. "To me there's a right way and a wrong way and medicine is free enterprise. I bet I make triple what you do."

"Probably so," I said. "But I make enough."

60

"You should come to Texas," he said. "In our business, you've got to go where the money is and now the money is here in Texas. This is where the rich are, and they're willing to pay to be beautiful."[1]

That exchange punctuates the contrast of Alexander MacDonald's allegiances with the ways of modern consumerist, individualistic, high-speed North American culture. It may be the author's commentary on Canadian medical professionals who, in recent years, have been heading south of the border for higher incomes. The book as a whole is about ties that go much deeper than chasing the highest salary, the greatest prestige, the most expensive playthings that the media touts and tries to get us to pursue as the evidence of success. It is a literary counterpoint to the proverbial tombstone whose sadly ironic epitaph reads: "He took care of himself." The story of Alexander MacDonald is told within an episode of family responsibility—specifically, of Alexander's love and care for his impoverished, sick, and alcoholic older brother, of giving up his time and his tenderness and his tears in honor of their common ancestry and in acknowledgment of their common humanity. The loyalties of which it speaks put the suggestion of moving to "where the money is" out of the question and, in fact, make it irrelevant. He scarcely *sees* the horizon of wealth and prestige that beckons so many people far away from homespun ties and responsibilities and heritage, because *his* focus is on a farther horizon *yet*—one of loyalty and kinship and compassion, one that involves living for others.

Contrast that with Luke's report of an episode in which Jesus was approached by one of two brothers, presumably the younger one, who by Jewish law was entitled to one-third of his father's estate compared with the older brother's two-thirds. But apparently, the older brother had taken control of the entire amount. "Someone in the crowd said to [Jesus], 'Teacher, tell my brother to divide the family inheritance with me'" (Luke 12:13). Jesus refused to be dragged into the family quarrel. He knew that the young man's interest was not really *justice*. "'Friend,'" he said, "'who set *me* to be a judge or arbitrator over *you*?'" (12:14). That's a warning to any of us not to presume that Jesus is on our side when we get into arguments with other people, even arguments about matters that *we* think have to do with fundamental right and wrong, religious or otherwise. Jesus keenly perceived that the *real* question, of course, wasn't about *justice*, but about *greed*, and not just about the greed of the *older* brother who had grabbed the entire inheritance, but *equally*, and since the man was standing right in front of

---

1. MacLeod, *No Great Mischief*, 59.

him, more *specifically*, the *younger* brother's greed that had prompted him to appeal to Jesus to enter the fray.

Perhaps the whole crowd had witnessed the incident and heard the younger brother's request. At any rate, Jesus used the occasion to warn all of those who were present,

> "Take care! Be on your guard against all kinds of greed; for one's life does not consist in the abundance of possessions." Then he told them a parable: "The land of a rich man produced abundantly. And he thought to himself, 'What should I do, for I have no place to store my crops?' Then he said, 'I will do this: I will pull down my barns and build larger ones, and there I will store all my grain and my goods. And I will say to my soul, "Soul, you have ample goods laid up for many years; relax, eat, drink, be merry."' But God said to him, 'You fool! This very night your life is being demanded of you. And the things you have prepared, whose will they be?'" (12:15–20)

The parable ends there, but Jesus said to the crowd, "So it is with those who store up treasures for themselves but are not rich toward God" (12:21). And he went on to tell his disciples—those who followed him—not to worry about things like food or clothing or even living long; *God* will provide the things that we *really* require. All that *we* need to do is to *trust* God and live in the way that *pleases* God. Those who genuinely follow Jesus will look to *God* for their security, not to their own ability to accumulate possessions and lay up wealth against the uncertainties of their earthly future. Life is not to be valued or measured in terms of dollars. "I bet I make triple what you do," the Texas orthodontist said to Alexander MacDonald. "Probably so," said Alexander MacDonald in return. "But I make enough."[2]

Did you notice that the rich man in Jesus' parable thought only about his own comfort and security? God had provided good seed and good soil in which to plant the seed, God had provided ample rain to water it and keep it luxuriant and make it fruitful, God had provided warm sunshine to cause it to germinate and grow and ripen. And when the harvest came in abundant to the point of bursting the man's barns, his immediate response was to stockpile it and devote the rest of his life to comfort, ease, and amusement—*all for himself*. He was not what anyone would consider to be a bad man. There is no suggestion that he was anything other than honest. Quite probably, he was hard-working. We need always to be cautious about embellishing the parables that Jesus told. But even without Jesus' saying so, his listeners would have been well aware that there were very few rich farmers

---

2. MacLeod, *No Great Mischief*, 59.

in those days who did not have servants to do most of the labor. And there are very few people in *any* age who do not have relatives and friends with various needs. And the *poor*, as Jesus said on another occasion, are *always* with us, and the *hungry*, as well. But the rich man's horizon of concern conspicuously encompassed no one but himself, his gratitude extended to no one but himself, and his interests clearly went no further than his own benefit. So, he said, "I will do this. I will pull down my barns and build larger ones, and there I will store all my grain and my goods. And I will say to my soul, 'Soul, you have ample goods laid up for many years; relax, eat, drink, be merry'" (Luke 12:18–19). Goods and prosperity were his only goal, and he had achieved them. Self-sufficiency was *his* definition of security, and so he could be proud of himself. Greed was his passion, and he had given himself completely to his lusty materialism. And that night he died. *Now*, to whom did all these things belong? The man's *actual* future was far different from what he had planned—all the ease, all the gluttony, all the merriment. And, we must surmise, when he unexpectedly found himself in the presence of God, God did not recognize him as one of God's own. The man was what we might call a "practical atheist." For, though he may have *professed* faith in *God*, in reality, he had never really *lived* a faith in *God*, but in *things*—in wealth and possessions.

Contrast that with the attitude of a man who lost his house and all his possessions to a wildfire driven by Santa Ana winds in Southern California not many years ago. When a television reporter shoved a camera and microphone in his face and asked him how he felt, the way that reporters do, he said that he and his brother had recently been talking about how they should be careful not to allow *their possessions* to possess *them*. Then, he announced triumphantly to the reporter, "I am a free man now!"—free to see beyond the pile of things that tend to clutter one's horizon and tempt us to focus on ourselves and make idols of our creaturely wants.

It seems that the Christian church at Colossae, in Asia Minor, had been hassled by some people who were teaching that, in order to achieve salvation, one needed to *deny earthly things* and the natural concerns of the *body*. The apostle Paul heard of it and wrote to the church to let the congregation know that they had it all backward. The point is, he said, for people who have been raised with Christ through the waters of baptism, that our natural interests are the things that have to do with *Christ*, who lives and reigns in heaven at the right hand of God. Our gaze should naturally be lifted from preoccupation with *ourselves* to concentration on the things that *Christ* summons us to do, the concerns that *Christ* calls us to think about, the goals that *Christ* sets before us—all having to do with the loving purposes of God, all having to do with restoring the wholeness of each person and all creation. That is not a matter of *denying* human needs—Jesus himself was daily involved in ministering to people by healing their diseases and satisfying their hunger and quenching their thirst and urging those who *have* to give to those who *have not*. But the new life that is ours as people who have *already* been raised with Christ is a life that has no idols. It does not set its focus on *things* or the pride that goes with them or drives us to go after them. The new life that is ours in Christ has as *its* vision the far horizon of heaven itself, and the way it stretches out toward that horizon is by doing all sorts of loving and generous deeds near at hand. The Colossian heretics, it seems, filled their vocabulary with spiritual phrases that advertised their piety in every sentence. But in their behavior, they had merely exchanged *one* set of legalisms for *another*, and they were more interested in imposing them on *others* than living by them *themselves*. Paul told them that giving up earthly preoccupations was fine, but that the deeper issues are evil desires and the selfish impulses of the human heart. Their denial of earthly things was so vocal and so loud that it was clear that, in fact, earthly things were still very much their focus. What they *really* needed to do was to allow Christ so to live within them and animate them and work his salvation through them that their daily lives would be totally transformed, and that the material world, through them, could be put to the service of heavenly purposes.

There was nothing wrong with the rich man's having an abundant harvest. The problem was what he *did* with his abundance (or *didn't* do with his abundance). The root of his greed was his failure to direct gratitude to the source of his blessing. When we forget where it all came from, we forget what it is for. And we and our desires end up occupying the center of our attention, become the focus of our lives, and that, Paul declares, is idolatry. And our vision of the heavenly horizon is spoiled by our physical excesses that use other people to satisfy our selfish appetites and by the unholy worship of our own wants, material and otherwise, that lead to anger, wrath, malice, slander, lying, and abuse. "If you have been raised with Christ," Paul says—and he is assuming that anyone who has been baptized *has* been raised with Christ—"seek the things that are above, where Christ is, seated at the right hand of God" (Col 3:1). Raise your eyes and your hopes to a *farther* horizon than the tight little circle of your own appetites. Lift your aspirations to a *higher* goal than relaxing, eating, drinking, and being merry. Be spiritual not just in speech or following a prideful legalism, but in living out the truth that Christ *is* all and *in* all. For our brother or our sister is not someone whom Christ exists to help us get something *from*. Our brother and our sister are the near-at-hand subjects through whom Jesus Christ, by our ministering to them generously and lovingly and selflessly, sharpens our focus on the far horizon of *heaven*, which is our new and eternal life in Jesus Christ.

NINETEENTH SUNDAY IN ORDINARY TIME
Spanish Springs Presbyterian Church, Sparks, Nevada
AUGUST 12, 2001

Isaiah 1:1, 10–20
Hebrews 11:1–3, 8–16
Luke 12:32–40

"The School of Hope"

Biblical scholars generally think that Israel, the Northern Kingdom of the Jews, already lay in ruins when this morning's Old Testament reading was written. The political and religious leaders' neglect of the poor and the oppressed, and their warping of worship into something that blessed their prejudices and sanctioned their pleasures rather than giving God's purposes a fair hearing, had already resulted in God's judgment upon Israel in the form of Assyrian soldiers and payments of tribute. Now, it was the turn of Judah, the Southern Kingdom, to face judgment. Would the people down south learn their lesson from what happened up north? Would they come to their senses? Would they remember God, and God's worthiness of their worship, and God's claim upon their loyalties and their attitudes and their behaviors? Oh, they certainly claimed to be faithful to God. They brought offerings. They burned incense. They had a calendar just *full* of holy days. But none of their public piety could paper over their private corruptions. And none of their individual prayers could mask their social injustices.

There was still an opportunity to win God's favor, though the door was already closing. "Wash yourselves," Isaiah pleaded as God's prophet,

> make yourselves clean;
>   remove the evil of your doings
>   from before my eyes;
> cease to do evil,

> learn to do good;
> seek justice,
> > rescue the oppressed,
> defend the orphan,
> > plead for the widow. (Isa 1:16–17)

If all these people who were so meticulously attentive to the ritual precision of their holy observances would just recover their genuine sense of awe before God their creator and heavenly king and gratefully remember the powerful *source* of their blessings as a nation and as individuals! If all these people who had reduced God to systems and doctrines would be humble enough to rejoice in the winsome love and utter dependability of the one who was as near to them as their breath! If all these people who paraded their purity would acknowledge *their* part in the greed and fear and excess of their society! If all these people who thought that security and prosperity had to do with weapons and alliances would trust the promises that God had made to their ancestors and had renewed through the prophets! If only Judah had a sense of awe, delight, truth, and hope, their prayers might be honest and their offerings could be genuine! Then, the catastrophe might be averted. Then, the judgment could be turned aside. Then, Judah's glaring sins could be washed pure as snow, white as wool. "If you are willing and obedient," the prophet declared,

> you shall eat the good of the land;
> but if you refuse and rebel,
> > you shall be devoured by the sword." (1:19–20)

Apparently, profit spoke more loudly than prophecy. Love of self was more intense than love of neighbor. Social injustices and private wrongdoings continued. Worship remained self-indulgent at worst and perfunctory at best. And, eventually, the Southern Kingdom fell to Babylon despite all the prophet's warnings, as the Northern Kingdom had fallen to Assyria. Judah refused God's fervent pleadings and rebelled against God's gracious authority and was, as Isaiah had predicted, "devoured by the sword" (1:20), for the warnings that Isaiah had spoken were the very words of God.

Repeatedly, not only in Isaiah, but in the other prophets, as well, neglect and abuse of the poor and the oppressed are stated as the reason for God's anger. And repeatedly, not only in Isaiah, but in the other prophets, as well, the neglect of the poor and the oppressed are tied to the corruption of worship. It must have made the people feel good to participate in religious spectacles, must have made them feel that they were doing their sacred duty that kept them right with God. But when what happened in their worship did not affect how they went about their public and private lives, did not influence their dealings with each other and with other nations, when the gracious generosity of God did not make any impression upon them in the way they regarded the poor, when the history of God's liberating redemption of the Hebrews from Egypt did not become their model of compassion toward the weak and the vulnerable, then God determined to get the lesson across in another way—by sending upon them conquering armies and economic ruin. Their worship was to be the school in which remembrance of God's love and mercy patterned all of their life. When their worship became something they did for their own satisfaction and their aesthetic contentment, when the words and the deeds and the music of the temple *stayed* in the temple and never found their way into the market or the dining room or the shop or the law court, the prophets began to hear the sound of thousands of feet marching in battle formation across the nation's borders.

But the prophets spoke not only of doom. Later in Isaiah, the prophecy turns again to the promises that God had made long ago to the ancestors—promises of wholeness, promises of restoration, promises of fruitfulness, promises of peace, promises of mercy, promises of salvation—promises that God would *remain faithful* to the purpose for which God had chosen a people in the *first* place, and given them a land of their own, and made of them a nation—promises that when God permits destruction, it is always in preparation for redemption, promises that when chaos threatens to reclaim what God has created, chaos will ultimately lose the contest, and God's will of unity and peace shall prevail. The faithfulness of God is the root of all true hope, and so the *people* of God are to be *messengers* of hope, not just in their *words*, but in their individual lives and their life together. And the Bible *declares* that all through their history, when the people put their hope in *God* rather than their *technologies*, when the people put their hope in *God* rather than their *weaponry*, when the people put their hope in *God* rather than their abilities to do for *themselves* better than what *God* has promised, that is when the people knew the *broadest* prosperity, the most *genuine* peace, the *least* anxiety, the *closest relationship* with God who created us to glorify God and to enjoy God forever.

The word "hope" has been trivialized in our time, misunderstood and misused to the point that it seems to many of us, perhaps, interchangeable with such words as "wish," "desire," even "craving" in the physical sense. It has come to be regarded as something dependent upon or even springing from human action and response. "I hope she calls tonight," we say. "I hope I get a new skateboard for my birthday." "I hope the roast isn't overdone." And even in the spiritual sense, a whole generation of Christians couldn't be blamed for confusing "hope" with "positive thinking" or "optimism" about particular outcomes of situations that are near at hand to us, because our *preachers* have often confused them.

Humanly speaking, everything seemed absolutely *hopeless* to the people of Judah when the Babylonian hammer finally fell. Isaiah and others had tried to call the people back to right worship of God, which emphatically meant also the right treatment of their neighbors, to live in the hope that ought to be *native* to children of God. When their fears and their greed and their selfishness caused them to persist in their insincere rituals and their unjust dealings, and God allowed the Babylonian armies to conquer them and carry them off into exile, Isaiah testified to God's unchanging purpose, tried to rekindle hope by encouraging faith in the God who had always been faithful, even when God chose to be a disciplinarian, even when God permitted natural and political and social forces to play out their inevitable consequences. If the loss of their military might and their inordinate riches caused them to *lose hope*, then the *focus* of their hope was wrong to begin with. It was on *things* rather than *God*. It was on *human abilities* rather than *divine promises*. It was lodged in *themselves*, weak and sinful and short-sighted, rather than in the one who is powerful enough to hold up a universe, holy enough to forgive evildoers, wise enough to see across eternity with perfect vision. Faith itself is the patient, enduring hope that looks forward to God's completion of all things and to our union with God at the end of our days. It has everything to do with the promises of God, and it is God's promises that are the root of our hope, it is God's promises that alone are worthy of our trust—promises that God will faithfully keep *regardless* of *our faithlessness*, promises that are true *regardless* of *our* choosing to *disbelieve* them, promises that honor God's purpose in creating the world and every living creature *regardless* of *our* ways that degrade the earth and treat others as objects, promises that are more real than all the things we see that terrify us and worry us and tempt us to think that what we can survey and acquire and count and use up is all there *is*.

One of the classes that I took on my study leave in July with Don Saliers, professor of theology and worship at Candler School of Theology, had as its principal text his recent book, *Worship Come to Its Senses*.[1] The play on words in the book title unfolds in the titles of its four chapters—"The Sense of Awe," "The Sense of Delight," "The Sense of Truth," and finally "The Sense of Hope"—all aspects of what ought to guide and result from our worship of God. These are things that the world and its culture do not teach us very well—awe, delight, truth, hope—certainly not in a pure and profound and abiding way. But all of these are what God expects of us and our *relationship*

---

1. Saliers, *Worship*.

with God, lived out in every moment of our lives, in each of our encounters with others, in each of our behaviors as a society.

Our culture of materialism and profit is founded on an advertising regime that tries not only through commercials but also through the popular music that we hear and the movies that we watch and the little boxed electronic worlds that we play with to persuade us that this *earthly* life is all that we *have* and so we must grab as much as possible even if it means not leaving others *enough*. We are daily being indoctrinated to get as much as we can *now* in the way of gadgets and amusement and the ultimate measure of worldly value—money—and so our culture ultimately promotes a sense of hopelessness by putting a premium on immediacy (before we change our minds), and possessions (which we can't take with us), and individualistic concerns (which tear at the harmony of creation).

In the midst of such a culture, genuine worship of God, its integrity, its consistency, is the school of hope. Genuine worship of God, its gestures, its hospitality, is the school of generosity. Genuine worship of God, its invitation, its inclusiveness, is the school of love. Genuine worship of God, its music, its silence, is the school of wonder. Genuine worship of God, its candor, its lament, is the school of honesty. Genuine worship of God, its words, its movements, is the school of grace. Genuine worship of God, its mercy, its assurances, is the school of peace. Genuine worship of God, its fairness, its kindness, is the school of justice. Genuine worship of God, its mutuality, its humility, is the school of joy that is much deeper than, and transcends, the shallow and instant gratifications that are the seductive stock and trade of pride and greed and self-love and self-deception. Genuine worship of God incorporates and nurtures a sense of awe, a sense of delight, a sense of truth, a sense of hope. It does not uncritically accept worldly obsessions and forms and conventions and maxims that would *deny* awe, that would *cheapen* delight, that would *undermine* truth, that would *defeat* hope. Instead, it stands over against them and offers an *alternative*, which is the vision of the kingdom of God that Jesus inaugurated. But paradoxically, genuine worship does not preoccupy us with an *other*-worldliness or divert us from the genuine needs of *this* world. Just the opposite—genuine worship involves us, because we learn and remember and practice the love and generosity and mercy and healing of God here in this place, in compassionate and self-giving care for the oppressed, the orphan, the widow—care for all of the weak and abused and forgotten and ridiculed and estranged, out there, in the world.

"How easy it is to forget to remember God in a culture of self-preoccupation and forgetful distraction," writes Don Saliers. "Remembering the hope by praising, thanking, confessing, and interceding is at the heart of Christian life. It is at the heart of Christian worship.... Without the living remembrance about the font, the book, and the table of Christ, there will be no worship in spirit and in truth.... Hope depends upon living memory made palpable."[2] In other words, hope depends upon our *worship* genuinely and authentically not only *recalling* but actually *experiencing together* the promises of God, and shaping our world in *conformity* to our worship, *acting upon* the promises of God in all of life. That can only happen when worship of God is engaged in with *no other purpose* than worshiping God.

"The community gathered and the community in service to neighbors near and far are but two sides of the same mystery of common life in Christ," Don Saliers writes near the end of his book.

> This is exactly what baptism and Eucharist point toward. Liturgy is not "playing church," but the formation and expression of God's grace in human form. Hope is always tempered with courage and realism, and thus kept from being mere optimism, wishful thinking, or utopian dreaming.
>
> ... [Authentic Christian worship] trains us for the reign of God yet to come. It arouses in us a passion for what the prophets spoke of: a time of justice and peace, a time of human reconciliation with God, a time of abundance and the healing of the nations.
>
> Our true hope lies in once again learning to join ... Jesus in ongoing *prayer and action in the world*.
>
> ... Authentic Christian worship, true to its sources and alert to the present realities of human life, is a school of hope.[3]

You have chosen to bring your hopes and fears to the place Christ promised to meet us—where two or three gather in his name about the book, the font, and the table. Class is in session. Welcome to the school of hope.

---

2. Saliers *Worship*, 68.
3. Saliers, *Worship*, 81–82, 85. Emphasis added.

Twentieth Sunday in Ordinary Time

Spanish Springs Presbyterian Church, Sparks, Nevada

August 19, 2001

Isaiah 5:1–7
Hebrews 11:29—12:2
Luke 12:49–56

"Fire on the Earth"

May I let you in on a professional secret? There are certain passages in the Bible that preachers rather wish weren't there. Some of them are very *difficult* to preach on. Some of them are rather *confusing* to preach on. Some of them are simply *embarrassing* to preach on.

Our Gospel reading from the lectionary this morning is one of those passages that I find very difficult, somewhat confusing, and a little embarrassing, and, frankly, my Bible would be a lot neater and tidier if it weren't there. As a matter of fact, my understanding of *Jesus* would be a little neater and tidier if it weren't there. "Do you think that I have come to bring peace to the earth?" (Luke 12:51a) Jesus asked the disciples one day. And, by including it in his Gospel, Luke understands Jesus to be asking the question of disciples of *every* age, including *us today*. To be honest, my first response to Jesus' question, and I think the first response of the *original* disciples to Jesus' question, was, "Yes, I *do* think that you have come to bring peace to the earth. At least I *did* think so—the Prince of Peace and all that, dying on the cross for my salvation and for the reconciliation of the world." And I would have thought that Jesus would be *pleased* with my answer, and I think the *original disciples* would have expected Jesus to be pleased with such an answer, too. But Jesus answered his own question before they could respond. "No, I tell you, but rather division!" (12:51b). And I, like the disciples before me surely must have been, am shocked and amazed.

"From now on five in one household will be divided, three against two and two against three; they will be divided:

> father against son
> and son against father,
> mother against daughter
> and daughter against mother,
> mother-in-law against her daughter-in-law
> and daughter-in-law against mother-in-law." (12:52–53)

And I, like the disciples before me surely must have thought, believe this sort of thing can't be good for evangelism and church growth. Who would want to follow a teacher and healer who promises division within one's own household, conflict in the family, dispute within the ranks? Did Jesus momentarily forget that he was supposed to be the door to the peaceable kingdom?

Then I remember the history of Christianity—how, in fact, families and friendships *were* divided by faith in Jesus Christ—those who *had* it and those who *didn't*, who were *jealous* of the time that a family member or a friend was spending with a new *church* family and engaging in worship and study and ministry of one kind or another, who regarded their friend's or family member's allegiance to the *heavenly king* as *disloyalty* to the *emperor* and neglect of the *ancient gods* an act of treason toward the nation, who felt *threatened* by the *new* code of attitude and behavior that a friend or family member had adopted, and who *couldn't imagine* worshiping or dining with people outside of one's social class, of a different nationality or ethnic background, of a condition or practice that respectable society had always regarded as *disreputable*. And I remember how nations have fought wars over matters of religion, and about how Christians have even fought wars against other *Christians* over matters of doctrine, and about all of the denominational splits, especially in America.

On the one hand, it is all evidence of just how seriously people have taken their understanding of Jesus' lordship and God's will over the years— that they would put loyalty to *Jesus* over loyalty to family and nation and job and class values and cultural norms. On the other hand, surely God does not desire *discord* in the world that was brought into being to exist in harmony with its Creator and with itself, and surely *Christ* does not want division in the *church* which he gave his life to establish and for which he still prays. And yet that is the way it has worked out. Could it be that neither God nor Jesus *desires* division and discord, but that both God and Jesus recognize that the penetrating light of truth *will result in* division and discord nevertheless? If so—and remember, the Gospel of Luke was written to assure the church at a time when it was suffering persecution and was in danger of suffering *more*, and puzzling over why *non*-Christians were hostile to the gospel and even cutting off relationships with their Christian friends and family members—then, this passage is still *difficult* to deal with, but less *confusing* and not so *embarrassing*. That the Word of God incarnate who came to heal the nations *has* prompted *divisions* among people is a fact that we all know. But the divisions are a sad reality of *human sinfulness*, not a cynical perversion of the *divine purpose*. Jesus, I think, was letting the disciples know what was *going* to happen, not saying that he *wanted* it to be that way. And the experience of the church in the centuries *since* then has borne out Jesus' sober prediction.

Maybe it was a truth that Jesus himself had learned during the course of *his* ministry, over the years of his faithful obedience to God. Maybe he had noticed, first with *dismay* and then with *resignation*, that a lot of people seem to take *offense* at forgiveness and wholeness and honesty, are actually too proud and too self-consumed to show mercy and to seek unity and to listen to the truth. I can imagine that he was not only *disappointed*, but *shocked* and *angry*, when the good people of his hometown drove him out of the synagogue and tried to throw him off a cliff; that he was later *dismayed* and *disgusted* when the scribes and Pharisees who presumed that they knew all about God and God's Messiah tried to test and trap him; and that he was finally *grieved* and *dejected* when the people of Jerusalem and even his followers turned against him and abandoned him, the Son of God whose very name means "Savior," to be arrested, tried, and put to death on the cross.

Maybe it was a coming to pass of what his impending death in Jerusalem signaled—in the end times, even the closest family ties would be dissolved, and the horrible injustice of the cross meant that the end time was starting. "I have a baptism with which to be baptized, and what stress I am under until it is completed!" (12:50) said Jesus, referring to the baptism of his suffering and death. His death would *expose* the divisions already *rending* creation, would make clear the *discord* that *inherently* exists between God and sinner, demand a *decision* of us whether we live to *gratify ourselves* or to *glorify God*, whether our allegiance is to the *creation* or to the *Creator*, whether we will worship *ourselves* or the one who brought us into being and provides for our needs. For no one can be faithful to the truth that Jesus spoke and did without being often at odds and sometimes at war with the world, even with dear friends and close relatives. Peace, in the sense of preserving the status quo of injustice and hatred and selfishness and greed and cruelty, must be at an end in Jesus Christ. He cannot tolerate it, much less bless it. It is peace that is no peace. And if *division* results from giving a living witness to the truth of God, giving a living witness to the *love* of

God, giving a living witness to the *claims* of God, then so be it. For the cost of maintaining a *false* peace in terms of lives lost and wasted is too great for the Prince of Peace to abide.

One has only to think of more modern examples of people who tried to bring real peace—Mahatma Gandhi, Martin Luther King Jr., Robert Kennedy, Anwar Sadat, Yitzhak Rabin—to see the depth of hatred that peacemakers can prompt and the violence, even death, that their words of reconciliation can spark. Nearly all of us can remember Prime Minister Rabin's assassination and his courageous actions that preceded it. Most of us can remember the price that Anwar Sadat paid for rising above ancient hatreds. Many of us remember the terrible spring of 1968. Some of us remember the killing of Mahatma Gandhi. We don't know the strains that their convictions caused within their families and their circle of friends. We know a lot more about the divisions within their societies, and the ultimate personal cost. And as World War II veterans are passing from the scene in increasing numbers, our attention is drawn to the defenders of truth who did *not* return from the battlefields, and the sword that pierced many a mother's heart in a war that had to be fought for the sake of genuine peace.

So, Jesus on his way to Jerusalem was becoming more aware of what would likely happen there, and likely happen to his disciples in the days and years and centuries to come, but was convinced that it was the will of God that he go—the God whose purpose is the reconciling unity of all creation to himself. And to accomplish that, there must be fire on the earth—the great revealing light of God's judgment upon all that lies at the *root* of discord, like envy and pride and greed and disrespect, the great purifying power of the truth, justice, and righteousness of God burning backfires against all lies and oppression and wickedness, the great emboldening force of the Holy Spirit turning hearts and changing minds and nerving wills to proclaim God's purpose of salvation and point to the kingdom with lives that are dedicated totally to following Jesus Christ, even to the cross. And as the fire of God's judgment and purity and zeal burns into our souls, and we commit ourselves completely to Jesus Christ, we will not be *surprised* when conflict arises as we change old patterns of life, as we shift our former allegiances, as we champion the truth, as we give witness to the will of God. Baptized with the Holy Spirit which came upon the disciples as tongues of fire, you and I are enlisted in the struggle for a peace which the world does not *want* but desperately *needs*, in the campaign for a hope which the world does not *understand* but *without* which it cannot *survive*, in the battle for freedom which everyone wants to define for him- or herself but which God, in appointing Jesus Christ as Lord, has defined for all of us. And forever and ever until the end of time, those who speak and do the truth of God can *expect*, though they must never *seek*, opposition and resistance, conflict and division.

The fire has been kindled in the life, death, and resurrection of Jesus Christ, and it has been fanned from sparks into flames by the coming of the Holy Spirit. "Do you think that I have come to bring peace to the earth?" (12:51a). If the world were not in *need* of Christ's peace, what *he did* would have caused no conflict at *all*, and what *we* do, when we are being faithful disciples, would cause no division. The fact that conflict and division arise when the Prince of Peace is heard through our faithful words and seen through our faithful deeds is *proof* of the *falsehood* of any *lesser* peace that the world already thinks it has. "I came to bring fire to the earth" (12:49a), said Jesus. And it is burning every time you and I share the earth's bounty with another, every time you and I forgive another's wrongs toward us, every time you and I heal another's disease, every time you and I lift another's burden, every time you and I feed another's hunger, every time you and I champion another's dignity, every time you and I offer another person hope in the name of Jesus Christ.

Twenty-first Sunday in Ordinary Time
Spanish Springs Presbyterian Church, Sparks, Nevada
August 26, 2001

Jeremiah 1:4–10
Hebrews 12:18–29
Luke 13:10–17

"Heaven on Earth"

Before it was converted into a mosque when the Ottoman Turks captured the city of Constantinople in 1453, the largest church building in the world was Hagia Sophia, "Holy Wisdom," built by the Emperor Justinian in the capital of his empire. The building still stands, though, in more recent years, it has been turned into a museum. Rising opposite the imperial palace, Hagia Sophia then, as it does now, soared above everything around it with a majesty and authority that made it seem to be the chief building of Constantinople, the city that is now called Istanbul.

The nave, the great room of the church where worshipers gathered, was originally a huge oval measuring 250 feet by 107 feet, and the side aisles made the overall dimensions 250 by 220 feet—larger than the area taken up by a football field. The nave was covered by a dome rising to 180 feet above the ground, all creating the impression of a vast enclosed space, made possible with an intricate series of supports designed and arranged so as to lift one's gaze from the ground up toward heaven, which the dome represented. The dome rested on forty-two arched windows, which seemed to detach the dome itself from the rest of the building.

The sixth-century writer Procopius said that all the various architectural elements seemed to come together in mid-air and float away from one another, each resting only on the part immediately next to it. The dome, he said, seemed not to rest on solid masonry at all, but appeared, rather, to be suspended by a golden chain from heaven. Not only the building itself but the interior decoration produced a transcendent spiritual effect—marbles from every part of the empire contributed their lovely and distinctive colors and veins, and were so well positioned that, according to one observer, the effect was as if there were meadows and flowers on the floor and the walls. But above everything else was the great dome, showing the cross outlined against a background of gold mosaic, and just below the dome were mosaic figures of seraphim, their wings spreading out like peacock feathers. Hanging oil lamps of gold, silver, and brass provided light that glinted off the shiny surfaces, including the gold-plated screen in front of the altar that depicted Christ, Mary his mother, and the apostles. Even the holy table was made of gold, inlaid with precious stones, and the vessels on it were solid gold, set with gems and pearls.

To the feeling of immense space and royal splendor there was joined a third impression—that of light. It seemed that the entire building was flooded with sunlight by day. The reflection of the sun from the marble, Procopius said, gave the sense that the church was not illuminated from any outside source, but that the sun's own radiance came to being within the church itself. By night, the thousands of lamps, hung at different levels, gave a brilliance in which there were no shadows anywhere. "Whenever anyone comes to the church to pray," Procopius wrote,

> he realizes at once that it is not by human power or skill, but by divine influence that this church has been so wonderfully built. His mind is lifted up on high to God, feeling that he cannot be far away but must love to dwell in this place he has chosen. And this does not happen only when one sees the church for the first time, but the same thing occurs to the visitor on each successive occasion, as if the sight were ever a new one. No one has ever had a surfeit of this spectacle, but when they are present in the building [they] rejoice in what they see, and when they are away from it, they take delight in talking of it.[1]

Another observer said of the lamps and the light they put forth: "[Whoever gazes on the light of the iconostasis, the screen in front of the altar], feels his heart warmed with joy; and looking on a lamp in the shape of a boat swathed with fire, or on some single lamp, or the symbol of the Divine Christ, all care vanishes from the mind, as when the wayfarer gazes on the stars of heaven.... Thus through the spaces of the great church come rays of light, expelling clouds of care, and filling the mind with joy."[2] He

---

1. Quoted in Downey, *Constantinople*, 112.
2. Quoted in Downey, *Constantinople*, 112.

said that at night, the light poured out of the windows and could be seen by sailors from their ships while they were still far out at sea, showing the way to travelers "as it shows the way to the living God."[3]

Hagia Sophia was the greatest building project of its time, but the designing of church buildings in the form of a square or a cross or an octagon surmounted by a great central dome was becoming standard in the East. The *dome* was the architectural *key*, unifying the whole building and bringing all of its areas and spaces to a single, central focus, a great hemisphere symbolizing heaven. The dome was visible, at least in part, to all worshipers in the church, binding the whole assembly together during their worship as one body of faithful, visible to each other in a place of majesty and dignity. They felt a serene sense of detachment from the world—a peace that could only be explained as experiencing heaven itself. And so, the great dome of Hagia Sophia and other churches of similar design seemed to bring heaven to earth. In this lofty vaulted space, the worshiper felt truly in touch with the communion of saints and the cloud of witnesses, and the community of the faithful on earth seemed very close indeed to those who had gone before. If you have ever been to one of these Greek Orthodox churches, ancient or modern, and heard the traditional chants reverberating and seen and smelled the incense rising up toward the heaven-like dome, you have perhaps had that same feeling.

Those who built Hagia Sophia understood that worship should be a foretaste of the kingdom of God. Every time Christians gather to give their praise, confess their sins, hear God's commands, offer their thanksgiving, pray for themselves and for the world, dedicate their treasures and pledge their abilities and their intentions, receive bread and wine from the Lord's table, and receive a blessing, it should be like a day in the kingdom of heaven. They believed that, as worship is the *spiritual* access into the direct presence of God that Jesus promised us, so worship should *physically* be an entrance into the *city* of the living God, the heavenly Jerusalem, majestic and lofty, and it should be a participation in the company of the saints who have already gone ahead of us, who dwell there eternally along with angels beyond number.

The members of the congregation to whom the preacher was speaking his sermon that *we* know as the letter to the Hebrews had once thought that the *law* was the only way to heaven—adhering to it strictly, and bringing sacrifices to be burned on the altar to atone for any *failures* to adhere to it strictly. Their worship was all about Mount Sinai—surrounded in clouds and smoke, trembling and quaking—on which Moses had received the

---

3. Quoted in Downey, *Constantinople*, 113.

Commandments from a God who could not be looked upon without the dread of death, so remote and unapproachable he is in his holiness, so unworthy and despicable we are in our sinfulness. Hebrews tells us, speaking of Sinai and the law that Sinai symbolizes, "'If even an animal touches the mountain, it shall be stoned to death.' Indeed, so terrifying was the sight that *Moses* said, 'I tremble with fear'" (Heb 12:20–21).

But in the death and resurrection of Christ, the blood of many goats and sheep and whatever else was required to be slaughtered upon the altar over and over again to make up for sin has been replaced by the once-for-all blood that Jesus shed on the cross. In Jesus Christ, the awe-full fear of the old covenant and Mount Sinai, as Hebrews puts it, a place of trembling and quaking, has been *replaced* with the *awe-filled joy* of the *new* covenant. So, our Christian worship is properly at Mount Zion, the city of the living God, an *unshakable* kingdom. "Therefore," says Hebrews, "since we are receiving a kingdom that cannot be shaken, let us give thanks, by which we offer to God an acceptable worship with reverence and awe" (12:28). Down at *Sinai*, as Thomas Long, professor of preaching and worship at Princeton Seminary, puts it, the blood of Abel "speaks a word of unfulfilled justice, but the only blood words spoken on *Zion* are *these*: 'This is my blood of the covenant, which is poured out for many for the forgiveness of sins.'"[4] The *perfect* sacrifice has already been made. The citizens of the heavenly city are thousands upon thousands of angels frolicking, laughing, festive, along with all those believers who have gone to their reward. As Professor Long puts it, perhaps exaggerating a little bit, Zion can be likened to the Sunday assembly of Christians praising and paying homage to God: "In heaven right now . . . there is a festive and ceaseless party underway, with angels fluttering around in joy and the saints swinging from the chandeliers. Every so often the floor of heaven opens up and this whole spree descends into ordinary time and space; this is Christian worship."[5]

It is more than a matter of architecture, of course, and in fact we know that the floor of heaven can open and we can worship God anywhere, even in a school cafeteria or a store-front, or without a building at all. But the great dome of Hagia Sophia and other Orthodox churches, and the depiction within it of the peaceful splendor of heaven, are meant to teach through the experience of *worship* something very *important* about God's *holiness*—that it is an invitation to live on high with God, whose kingdom is peace and majesty and joy and beauty and light, whose grace is lavish, whose forgiveness is complete, whose love is everlasting. And every time we enter

---

4. Long, *Hebrews*, 139. Emphasis added.
5. Long, *Hebrews*, 138.

the door of a sanctuary, be it a huge cathedral or a humble house-church, what we experience there, not only in the words of scripture and liturgy but in the worshipers' own mutual gestures of love and acceptance and their own expressions of forgiveness and encouragement and their own sense of unity and joy, should be like a day in heaven. But *unlike* the Greek Orthodox emphasis, we in the Reformed Protestant tradition see in scripture not a mandate for worship to *detach* us from the cares of the world, but to *present* them to *God* and to *commit ourselves* to *address* them through *ministry* in the way that God's own Son did. Christian worship must testify not only that *we* are raised to *heaven*, but that *God* stoops down to *earth* in the person of *Jesus Christ*. Worship is not about lifting us out of life's daily realities. Worship is a celebration of the good news that God has plunged into them. The glory of the sanctuary is not that God sits on the top of Mount Sinai, shrouded in clouds and smoke and daring us to approach the divine throne. The glory of the sanctuary is that God's Son gives himself to us at the table, and that the Holy Spirit binds us together as one with each other and with the saints of all the ages.

One sabbath, Jesus was worshiping in a synagogue, listening intently, no doubt, to the reading of the law and the warnings and promises of the prophets about God's intention that Israel be a nation of justice and righteousness, of truth and compassion. Suddenly, a woman came into the synagogue—scandalous in itself—a woman who was crippled—yet another scandal. When Jesus saw her there in her bent-over condition, he called to her—scandal number three—and pronounced her free from her ailment—an additional scandal. For the synagogue, the place of worshiping God in the local village, was a place for men only, and only for men who were ritually pure (including being free of disease or deformity). Men were not supposed to speak to women directly, but only through their husbands. And what human being could presume to do what only *God* had the right to do—forgive and heal? And then, breaking yet another taboo, Jesus touched her—again, something that a man must not do. And to top it off, this all happened on the sabbath, when even the smallest chores were strictly limited and great works like healing were forbidden altogether.

The others there thought that worship was supposed to be about acknowledging the cloud and the smoke on Mount Sinai, focused only on the holy and *unapproachable* God, a turning away from the sins and ailments and ugly realities of life on earth.

> The leader of the synagogue, indignant because Jesus had cured on the sabbath, kept saying to the crowd, "There are six days on which work ought to be done; come on *those* days and be cured,

and *not* on the *sabbath* day." But the Lord answered him and said, "You hypocrites! Does not each of you on the sabbath untie his ox or his donkey from the manger, and lead it away to give it water? And ought not *this woman*, a daughter of Abraham whom Satan bound for *eighteen long years*, be set *free* from *this* bondage on the *sabbath day*?" (Luke 13:14–16)

At that moment, it seems, that synagogue ceased to be a symbol of Mount Sinai, an experience of God's awful terror, and became a symbol of Mount Zion, an experience of the joyful kingdom of heaven. The woman's long ailment, which the people would have considered to be a consequence of sin, could not be allowed to bind and cripple her in the kingdom of heaven. And in the presence of Jesus Christ, she was in the very *midst* of the kingdom of heaven. "When [Jesus had spoken], all his opponents were put to shame; and the entire crowd was rejoicing at all the wonderful things that he was doing" (13:17). There is no sorrow or pain in heaven. In heaven, burdens have been lifted and suffering has been ministered to. The entire crowd is rejoicing at all the wonderful things that God is doing in Jesus Christ—forgiveness and wholeness, awe and wonder, joy and peace, community and salvation, no shadows of fear or guilt, but the bright shining Light of the World alive and at work in their midst. That is what worship is about. Because that is what the kingdom of heaven is like. And worship, as those who built Hagia Sophia long ago understood, should be an experience of heaven on earth.

Twenty-second Sunday in Ordinary Time
Spanish Springs Presbyterian Church, Sparks, Nevada
August 29, 2010

Jeremiah 2:4–13
Hebrews 13:1–8, 15–16
Luke 14:1, 7–14

"The Trouble with Angels"

Many people are fascinated with angels. Hardly anything in the Bible stimulates the imagination so much. But it's also true that most people don't really know much about what the Bible says concerning angels. Unfortunately, our popular notions are formed quite as much by movies and greeting cards and figurines as by scripture. And when someone tries to comfort a grieving parent with a statement like, "God must have needed another angel," it diverts attention from the *real* promises of God contained in the Bible and can result in either mushy faith or anger at God. The Hebrew word often translated as "angel" in the Old Testament and elsewhere is related to the verb that means "to send." By implication, then, the chief attribute of an "angel" in the Old Testament is of being *sent*, as with a *message*. The same is true of the Greek term that appears in the New Testament, "angelos."

In the English biblical translation, angels are typically regarded as *spiritual* beings, but, on their face, the Hebrew and Greek words used for such beings in the Old and New Testaments imply that angels can be either *human* or *heavenly*. The Apocrypha even *names* some of the angels, as do the Old Testament book of Daniel and the New Testament books Luke, Jude, and 1 Thessalonians. The nature and role of angels is described in various ways in the Bible, but they are always in some manner connected to God, or to heaven, although the Bible nowhere says that they can or do *fly*. They can come to earth as God's servants to accomplish specific tasks, frequently to sustain human beings who are *also* serving God in particular ways—like the angel that fed Elijah when he was hiding out on Mount Horeb and the angels that ministered to Jesus in the wilderness—and, even though conceived as heavenly in origin, they are often indistinguishable from human beings. One thing is always clear in the scriptures, though: while it is sometimes inferred that they are immortal, angels are *created* beings, not gods in any sense, although they do God's bidding. They are not to be *worshiped*, but, instead, *they* worship *God*. And that means that even heavenly angels are not so different in character from men and women who are faithful to God. Sometimes, they are thought of as forming a sort of heavenly council that God consults about various matters. Sometimes, they are imagined as constituting a mighty army marching under God's orders. There are many references to angels in the New Testament, where they play an important role at specific points in the stories of the Gospels and Revelation and in Hebrews. Satan is sometimes spoken of as the leader of the fallen angels, which suggests that, though they exist to serve God, angels also have the capacity to make their own bad choices and to work in ways that are contrary to God's purposes. None of them is a perfect reflection of God, as Jesus Christ is.

All of that seems confusing and heightens the appeal of more simplistic portrayals of angels for a lot of folk, both serious Christians and people who only dabble in things religious. But the *Bible* is *our* standard for learning about the things of God, not Hallmark and not Frank Capra. The *Bible* rather takes their existence for granted without explaining them in detail, and maybe *we* should be content to accept their existence and the possibility that they are presently active in the world without speculating about them or insisting on particular beliefs about them as an article of faith. In any event, it is best for us to follow the Bible's lead in allowing angels to remain somewhat mysterious.

One activity related to the appearance of angels is the custom of showing hospitality to strangers. You will remember that Abraham received some strangers, assumed to be angels, who conveyed to him the message that he and Sarah, though aged, would have a child so that God's promise of a great number of descendants would be possible. Even before he knew who they were or had received their message, Abraham instructed Sarah his wife to make cakes of bread for the visitors, and he himself selected a calf from his herd with which to feed them and set milk and curds before them (good eating by ancient standards). On another occasion in Genesis, angels visiting Sodom were treated inhospitably by the citizens, with the result that Sodom was destroyed, excepting only Lot and his family, for Lot *had* treated them as guests who deserved to be cared for and sheltered from harm. And in the final chapter of Hebrews, which is a list of admonitions and encouragements to behave in a way consistent with the dispositions of faith, hope, and love, we read, "Do not neglect to show hospitality to strangers, for by doing that some have entertained angels without knowing it" (Heb 13:2). The Greek word for hospitality here literally means "love for guests," the word "guest" being derived from the word for "stranger," "foreigner," "alien." Except for the mention of angels, we might well read over that verse without thinking a great deal about it. Like showing mutual love, and like remembering and visiting those who are in prison, teaching about hospitality is not unique to Hebrews. But the specific *rationale* for opening up one's home and one's table to strangers heightens our interest and, if you will, raises the stakes of our obedience. Remember what happened to Sodom—surely the original hearers of Hebrews were well aware!

Many commentaries make a point of saying that the "guests" anticipated in Hebrews were obviously Christian travelers, perhaps itinerant evangelists who wouldn't want to lodge at inns, which had a reputation for shady activities, besides, of course, being expensive. But the Bible itself doesn't really limit the sort of guests to whom Christians owe hospitality, the sort of guests who should be welcomed under one's roof and served at one's table. And if we think that we are justified in qualifying in any way the sort of people whom we *will* welcome under *our* roof and serve at *our* table, we aren't even living up to the common standards of generosity by which *non*-Jews and *non*-Christians lived in the ancient Near East. Surely the people of God can do better than that! And yet, in our security-conscious, hygiene-conscious, convenience-conscious, reputation-conscious culture, not many of us are willing to show real hospitality to a genuine stranger, and I, your pastor, confess that I am among them. I have little reluctance to receive the stranger, the foreigner, the alien, under our *national* roof or at our *national* table—that's what the Statue of Liberty is about, isn't it? I have rather more reluctance welcoming under our *church* roof and at our *church* table someone who looks, sounds, and behaves very different from myself—a reluctance of which I am ashamed. And I have even *more* reluctance welcoming the total stranger into my *home* and to the *family* dinner table—hardly the proper attitude for a follower of Christ, who was born in a stable because there was no room in the inn and who, having been labeled a criminal, was buried in a borrowed tomb. Would it change our attitude if we really believed what the Bible says—that the stranger who seeks our hospitality, seeks to be our guest, might in fact be an *angel*, might be God's *agent*, might have an important *message* for us from the Creator of the universe?

Luke tells of an occasion on which Jesus had been invited to the house of a leader of the Pharisees to eat a meal on the sabbath. He already had enemies, and they were watching closely to see whether they could catch him in any breach of law or etiquette. Jesus noticed how some in attendance took for granted their importance and prestige, sat as a matter of entitlement near their host. It was the custom for the wealthier, more esteemed guests to take a position at or near the head table at a banquet so that the other guests could see for themselves how important they were. But Jesus, perhaps remembering a passage from Proverbs on that subject—

> Do not put yourself forward in the king's presence
> or stand in the place of the great;
> for it is better to be told, "Come up here,"
> than to be put lower in the presence of a noble (Prov 25:6–7)—

told them what Luke describes as "a parable" (maybe because Jesus referred to a hypothetical wedding banquet rather than that specific sabbath dinner). "When you are invited by someone to a wedding banquet, do not sit down at the place of honor, in case someone more distinguished than you has been invited by your host; and the host who invited both of you may come and say to you, 'Give *this* person *your* place,' and then in disgrace you would start to take the *lowest* place. But when *you* are invited, go and sit down at the *lowest* place, so that when your host comes, he may say to you, 'Friend, move up higher'; then you will be honored in the presence of all who sit at the table with you" (Luke 14:8–10). That is nothing more than good practical advice, really. But, calling it a parable, Luke understood that it had to do with one's relationship to God: "For all who exalt themselves will be humbled, and those who humble themselves will be exalted" (14:11).

Then Jesus turned from the way one should be a *guest* to the way one should be a *host*. "He said also to the one who had invited him, 'When you give a luncheon or a dinner, do not invite your friends or your brothers or your relatives or rich neighbors, in case they may invite you in return, and you would be repaid. But when *you* give a banquet, invite the poor, the crippled, the lame, and the blind. And you will be blessed, because they cannot repay you, for you will be repaid at the resurrection of the righteous'" (14:12–14). Clearly, Jesus is not talking only about itinerant preachers. Jesus is defining real hospitality, of which there is precious little in our modern Western world and of which there was apparently no over-abundance in his own time and place. The other people gathered at the house of the Pharisee leader that day probably didn't know anyone such as Jesus was talking about. Of course, we think of Jesus' own willingness to associate with and minister to, even eat with and touch, the poor, the crippled, the lame, and the blind. Jesus was, in short, encouraging the leader of the Pharisees to be like Jesus himself.

Now, why were the other guests in the house that day along with Jesus "watching him closely" (14:1)? For the *very* reason that *he* had been associating with and ministering to, even eating with and touching, the poor, the crippled, the lame, and the blind! Jesus knew that. But instead of offering a *defense* of *his* activity, he told his Pharisee host, in the presence of his guests, that *he* should be doing the same thing! Free yourself from the pressure of always needing to feel you are number one! Stop having always to compare yourself with others, devaluing them so that you can feel superior! Spend yourself in unconditional generosity, not calculating the return on your investment of inviting only the right people! The only accurate source of honor and identity and position is God, and God cares not a whit about how much we make, only how freely we give; cares not a whit about how tidy is our appearance, only how compassionate are our hearts; cares not a whit about the placement of knives and forks and spoons and dishes and glasses, only that the poor and the crippled and the lame and the blind receive a full share of the earth's goodness, and a full share of our attention and fellowship, to *all* of which God says they are entitled. And what may we *learn* from such guests? What message of trust in God, what message of love for our fellow creatures, what message of unconditional mercy and grace which, having ourselves received as an undeserved blessing, we are to multiply and pass on as blessings to others? "Do not neglect to show hospitality to strangers, for by doing *that* some have entertained angels"—messengers from God—"without knowing it" (Heb 13:2).

That's the trouble with angels. They come sometimes at inconvenient times. They come sometimes in apparel that we don't recognize from the greeting cards and the paintings and the figurines. They even come sometimes unshaven, with teeth missing, smelling of the alley and the dumpster rather than the perfumed hallways of heaven. They may seem rude, by our standards, not polished in their manners nor advanced in their education. They may seem unworthy of our compassionate attention because, hungry and looking for work and without any prospects of feeding their families, they have come to where they think they might get a job, even though it's against the law to be here. They may even seem not to be Christians, at least not in the sense of sitting regularly in the pew and depositing regularly in the plate and speaking regularly in the vocabulary of scripture. Of course, if they *did*, we might hasten to entertain *them* to the exclusion of *others* who are genuinely in *need* of hospitality. "Do not neglect to show hospitality to strangers, for by doing that some have entertained angels without *knowing* it" (13:2). That's the trouble with angels.

Twenty-third Sunday in Ordinary Time

First Presbyterian Church, Dodge City, Kansas

September 6, 1998

Jeremiah 18:1–11
Philemon 1–21
Luke 14:25–33

"Pray, and Do the Right Thing"

As we have been reading through Luke's Gospel this summer, we have heard Jesus respond to individuals, to his disciples, to other small groups of people—even Pharisees—who have come asking him questions. All this time, he has been traveling the road to Jerusalem, and Luke reminds us of that fact in little editorial parentheses now and then. The author wants us always to bear in mind that what Jesus says in these chapters—what he teaches and what he commands—must be understood against the backdrop of Jesus' own journey toward Jerusalem, toward the Upper Room, toward Gethsemane, toward the judgment hall, toward Calvary, and toward the cross. He is issuing a call to discipleship that requires an immediate hearing and an immediate response. There is an *urgency* about what Jesus says; he is not merely making suggestions for happier living, he is not just offering proposals for casual discussion. There is a *poignancy* about what Jesus says; he will soon test his own words about trust and obedience and faithfulness in the most radical act of trust and obedience and faithfulness that the world has ever known. There is a *paradox* about what Jesus says; with every step he takes nearer to his *own death*, he is offering the most convincing evidence for the only manner in which any of *us* can have *genuine life*.

Today, we read of a new circumstance as Jesus continues his journey toward his execution. No longer is he dealing with just a *handful* of folk, but *huge multitudes* have joined in the walk toward the great city, almost like a parade, it seems, with the atmosphere of a joyful outing—a picnic, perhaps, or a circus, for in Jerusalem, surely, the priests will welcome Jesus and congratulate all his followers, or Jesus will foment a revolution against the Romans and his followers will win the day, or some great miracle will happen and all will be well. But we who have been reading through Luke's Gospel know that it is no picnic, it is no circus. We know that Jesus is on his way to his death. And with every village Jesus goes through and every hill that Jesus climbs over, there grows ever more distinct on the horizon the silhouette of the cross.

Conscious of his destiny, but suspecting also that most of the crowd was oblivious to the costs of discipleship, unaware of the risks involved in being his followers, Jesus told them bluntly: "Whoever comes to me and does not hate father and mother, wife and children, brothers and sisters, yes, and even life itself, cannot be my disciple. Whoever does not carry the cross and follow me cannot be my disciple . . . . [N]one of you can become my disciple if you do not give up all your possessions" (Luke 14:26–27, 33). Now the word "hate" here does not mean to loath or despise. In the language of the ancient Jews, it meant to turn away from, or to detach oneself from, someone or something. Jesus wanted those in the crowd who would follow him, and the disciples who were *already* following him, to understand that loyalty to him can and will create tensions within oneself and between oneself and those one loves, and that in any *conflict* of *loyalties* between Jesus and possessions, Jesus and family, or Jesus and nation, loyalty to Jesus must be primary, loyalty to Jesus must remain undiluted, loyalty to Jesus must emerge absolute. That being the case, everyone must consider what *price* he or she is willing to *pay* in obedience to the call of Christ.

Most of you know that I have a particular interest in Dietrich Bonhoeffer and have attended seminars on his life and thought over the years, including one just a few weeks ago. The twentieth century produced no keener theological mind, no larger compassionate heart, no more committed ecumenical voice, no more provocative ethical spirit, than Dietrich Bonhoeffer. And it certainly produced no more dramatic witness to Jesus Christ. Just as he was embarking upon his theological career in Germany, the Nazis came to power. He and his family became active in the German resistance, were instrumental in transporting Jews to safety, helped to establish the German Confessing Church as an alternative to the government-controlled state church, and participated in a plot to assassinate Hitler. For this, Bonhoeffer was eventually imprisoned, and, ultimately, he was hanged in one of Hitler's last acts of vengeful rage.

Bonhoeffer's many writings are powerful, but intrigue with the man himself comes not merely from his words but from his manner of living. If it impresses someone like me, who first read his book *The Cost of Discipleship* twenty-five years ago, how much *more* impact he had on the lives of those who knew him personally—some of whom I have been privileged to meet at these various seminars—his best friend, Eberhard Bethge; his niece Renate; one of his seminary students, Albrech Schönherr, formerly a Lutheran bishop in communist East Germany. One of the fascinating things that all of these people emphasize is the manner in which this amazingly complex young man Dietrich Bonhoeffer lived with a simple focus: praying, and participating in the sufferings of God. "It is evident," Bonhoeffer wrote in his unfinished book, *Ethics*, "that the only appropriate conduct of [people] before God is the doing of His will. The sermon on the mount is there for the purpose of being done. Only in *doing* can there be submission to the will of God."[1] Not in *judging* one's fellows and their moral failings—that is to usurp *God's* role—but in doing *ourselves* what *God wants—that* is being *faithful*. Bonhoeffer said, "Action is and must continue to be the only possible attitude towards the law of God."[2] There was a lot of *talk* about God in Nazi Germany, about how God favored the German people, about how it was God's will that Germany should triumph in its battles, about how the Nazi program and values were based on Christian principles, but the genuine Word of God—the Word of human compassion, the Word of sincere peace, the Word of inclusive blessing, the Word of humble gratitude, the Word of abundant mercy, the Word of the cross—was missing from the political rhetoric, and soon it was absent from people's thoughts.

With the church shackled and the gospel corrupted and God's truth censured as perhaps never since the earliest days of Christianity, Bonhoeffer wrote that the modern Christian must exercise his and her faith in the rhythm and pattern of praying and doing justice. By "praying," he meant not just speaking the words, but living the sort of life that nurtures discipleship, especially by participating in a small group of committed Christians who pray for one another, who encourage one another, who study with one another, who together concentrate on the Christian disciplines—not Sunday morning mass exercises in self-congratulation or sentimentality, not loud rallies, not bumper stickers, not slick Christianity, but mutual nurturing of an intense loyalty to Christ. By "doing justice," he meant actively responding to Christ's command, righteous action rather than self-righteous talk, the concrete deed rather than the abstract discussion, answering the urgent call to discipleship immediately by being born again daily, each moment, as *we* do what Christ would *have* us do. Bonhoeffer's German phrasing at this

---

1. Bonhoeffer, *Ethics*, 43.
2. Bonhoeffer, *Ethics*, 45.

point is difficult to render into English, but the sense can best be suggested by the charge to pray and do the right thing.

As the days are running out on Bonhoeffer's century, we find that the forces of modernity at work in the world as *he* knew it are still influential today. They may not be as blatant as in Nazi Germany—the exalting of the state that would make even the *church* an organ of propaganda, claims to ethnic and national superiority that produce intolerance and prejudice, a celebration of human ingenuity which crowds out the freedom of the human spirit—but they are still with us. We see their tracks in the destruction of community by individualism run rampant, in the assertion of human mastery over everything that *rivals* human power (including even nature itself), in intentional genocide and in murder by neglect, in lust for material gain which only widens the immoral gap between the haves and the have-nots. And so, Bonhoeffer's exhortation to pray and do the right thing—to discern who Christ is for us, today, and envision what he is calling us to do at this very moment, and then to act accordingly, without flinching and without excuse—this remains the basic ethical task of every Christian in the 1990s as in the 1940s. And the risk of opening ourselves up to the costliness of obedient discipleship—the cost to income, to family ties, to reputation, even to life itself—is as great for us as it was for that first generation of Christians, and *must* be, or ours is an empty faith, the shallowness of a vow unsupported by loyalty and the contradiction of a commitment ungirded by the will to sacrifice.

Long centuries before Dietrich Bonhoeffer was compelled to calculate the costs of *his* discipleship and to take the risky steps which resulted in freedom for a handful of Jews and pitted him against the Nazi authorities and led him to sober prayer for the defeat of his own country and the repugnant necessity of planning the murder of its leader, the drama of hearing and responding to Christ's call was played out on a much smaller stage in the town of Colossae in Asia Minor. The occasion was of less historic import—more on the scale that most of *us* will find *ourselves* tested in *our* faith—but it was no less a moment calling for prayer and doing the right thing. In a time and place in which a human life could be considered an item of exchange—something to be bought and sold—an apostle of Jesus Christ had taken a special interest in a slave who had come to him, we are not sure how—as a runaway or on some authorized mission—but providentially, as the apostle interpreted it. From a prison cell, probably in Ephesus, the apostle wrote to the slave's owner in Colossae. He beseeched him to forgive the slave for any inconvenience or expense that he had caused by running away or dallying too long on his errand, and to receive him back no longer as a slave, but as a Christian brother, no longer a commodity, but a person whom Jesus loved and for whom Jesus died. "I am sending him, that is, my own heart, back to you. I wanted to keep him with me . . . but I preferred to do nothing without your consent, in order that your good deed might be voluntary and not something forced. . . . [W]elcome him as you would welcome me" (Phlm 12–14, 17b), he urged the slave's owner. Would this professed follower of Jesus Christ have the strength to set aside his anger? Would he have the conviction to disregard his financial investment and the daring to act upon his declared loyalty to the one who lived for others and died so that others might live? "Pray," Paul was saying to the owner of the slave Onesimus, "and do the right thing."

Ultimately, that is the agenda of the Christian life. It has a simple sound to it, and yet the effect is to wrench a man or a woman or a child away from every worldly *security* and to *pit* a man or a woman or a child against every worldly *value*. It means that the follower of Christ must put loyalty to *him* above every loyalty to family or job or nation, every financial interest, every personal prejudice, every prideful thought, for at some time or other, they will all try to seduce us from doing what Christ requires, maybe even by appealing to us in the name of God's will and under color of Christian values. Jesus advised the throng crowding around him, "I require your absolute allegiance—an allegiance that will mean that you must act, and act in disregard of every *other* loyalty and every *other* desire. At the end of this road I walk, there looms a cross, and it is silhouetted against the horizon of everyone who walks this road with me. Now sit down and decide if you are willing to pay that price. If so, I call you to be my disciple—to pray, and do the right thing."

Twenty-fourth Sunday in Ordinary Time
Spanish Springs Presbyterian Church, Sparks, Nevada
September 12, 2004

Jeremiah 4:11–12, 22–28
1 Timothy 1:12–17
Luke 15:1–10

"Dinner Will Be Late"

The guests began arriving early. Some of them, those who traveled on foot, had set out almost as soon as they had received their invitation. In fact, they very nearly had to, it had been delivered such a short time before the appointed hour. But, of course, most people were quite willing to drop what they were doing, for such an invitation was to be coveted. The big house up on the hill—who hadn't wanted to see inside the beautiful carved doors, inside the impressive stone walls, inside the leaded glass windows that glinted in the early morning and late afternoon sun as they reflected the dawn and the sunset? There were rumors of what sumptuous feasts were served there, and now they would have their own opportunity to taste of the most magnificent dinner. But none of those things was as important in the minds of the invited dinner guests as the opportunity to be in the presence of their host.

It was not the social event of the *season*. It was the social event of a *lifetime*. And so most people had immediately sent their reply that, yes, they would indeed be present, even though it meant canceling other appointments or plans, even though it meant searching rapidly through the closet for something appropriate to wear, even though it meant disappointing some other dinner host or disappointing the guests they had invited to their own dinner tables that evening; as it turned out, *they* had all been invited to the big house on the hill, too, and so the prospective hosts and guests of other dinner parties were all somewhat relieved to have an excuse for breaking their previous engagements. Some very few had thought it not worth the trouble, or for some strange reason known only to them, had never had an interest in dining at the big house on the hill. *Most* of the community couldn't imagine being anyplace *else* once the invitations had been issued. Quite a few of them had never dreamed of ever *receiving* such an invitation. Then there were other people like Mr. Self, who secretly wondered why it had taken so long—his whole lifetime—to be invited to dinner at the big house on the hill.

Tobias Self, in fact, was unaware that anyone else had been invited to the meal. He supposed that the honor was his alone. And quite naturally so—his host, it seemed to him, had finally taken notice of the outstanding and honorable individual that he was, had finally recognized the egregious social oversight of not having invited him to dinner long before this, *long before this*. Now, as he looked in the mirror in his dressing-room, he adjusted his bowtie so that it was centered perfectly and examined his neatly parted hair to be certain that not a single strand was out of place. He seldom wore his tuxedo; few functions in this village were really appropriate for such dress, but he had taken rather for granted that the dinner party in the big house on the hill would be just such an occasion. He glanced at the clock on the wall. Six-thirty o'clock. He rang for his house-servant, Mr. Hobbs, who appeared promptly at the door to his dressing room.

"Is the carriage at the door?" he asked, giving a final, critical, but ultimately approving look in the mirror.

"Yes, sir," the servant responded.

"Very good," answered Mr. Self. "I shall be out most likely the entire evening."

"Very good, sir," the servant replied.

"In fact, Mr. Hobbs, you may have the night off," added Mr. Self, feeling in a generous mood.

"Oh, thank you very much, sir," said the servant. He followed Mr. Self down the stairs and then hastened ahead of him to open the front door, bowing as Mr. Self strode past him into the cool evening air.

The sun had just set, but the last beams of daylight illumined the big house on the hill and glinted off the west-facing windows. Mr. Self, who was always punctual and especially desired to be punctual this evening, had calculated the time it would take for his carriage to wind along the forested lane that led from the village up to the hilltop, roughly twenty minutes. "You know our destination, driver," he said, half inquiring and half confirming as he climbed into the brougham carriage past the man who held the carriage door open for him.

"Yes, indeed, sir," said the coachman, who closed the door behind Mr. Self and then climbed up to the driver's seat and took the reins of the horse. "Gi, gi," he clicked his tongue at the horse, who came to life and started forward with a little jolt.

Fortunately, it was not a breezy evening; Mr. Self's top hat and cape were quite unnecessary at the moment, merely a part of the wardrobe, but it would be colder after dinner, for there was a noticeable touch of fall in the air, and long-time locals had been speculating whether there might be an early snowstorm this year. Indeed, heavy clouds were now starting to move in from the northwest. Mr. Self could see them out the left window of the brougham as the carriage started its climb up from the valley floor toward the big house. But more noticeable than the clouds in the sky were the people on the road, most of them on foot, some on horseback, a few in other carriages. He tapped on the roof of the brougham with his cane, and the driver opened the little trap door behind his seat. "What is this? What are all these people doing?" Mr. Self asked, his voice expressing genuine inquisitiveness rather than displeasure.

"Sir, they seem to be headed toward the same destination as we. I'm afraid we may be a little late, sir, owing to the number of people walking on the road."

"Oh, I very much desire not to be late," Mr. Self grumbled, more to himself than to the coachman. "Can you not ask them to step aside?"

"They go on as far as I can see, sir," the coachman replied. "There must be fair a hundred of them."

"And are they all going in our direction? Toward the big house, I mean?"

"Yes sir."

Mr. Self tried to think what sort of event could be drawing a crowd out along the lane. There were no fields along this road for a sporting contest—what would it be in the dark, anyway?—and there really was no other possible destination to which they would be headed—only the big house at the top of the hill.

Mr. Self was quite puzzled. Then a happy thought occurred to him. Perhaps, yes, it was the only explanation, his host was throwing a grand dinner in his honor, recognizing his outstanding example for the community, a surprise affair. Mr. Self's eyes moistened to think of all these folk from the village coming up the long road to greet him. Some of them, he would not have thought would have cared, really. There were, after all, some rough and unsophisticated people in the crowd that surrounded his carriage. He recognized most of them, had seen them in the village even if he never had any dealings with them. Even now, they were not paying any particular attention to the brougham or its passenger, though the curtains were drawn back and he was clearly visible to anyone passing by.

Just then, Mr. Self recognized the village's tax assessor and collector drawing up even with the carriage on horseback. Had his host really invited *him*? Well, he *was* important, in a disagreeable sort of way. He began to look more carefully at the travelers along the road, judging what sort of people they were from their clothes and, in some cases, their make-up, and, in some cases, their odor, like the smell of cheap, heavy perfume emanating from two women wearing bright red lipstick and dresses quite unsuitable, in Mr. Self's judgment, to a dinner party. *Some* people, he then noticed, were dressed in tatters—old clothes, dirty clothes, the clothes of beggars, the clothes of orphans. He had passed them by on the streets of the village from time to time. Here, one was limping. There, one was even being carried on a stretcher. Mr. Self reached into the inside pocket of his tuxedo jacket and pulled out the printed invitation. He tapped again on the roof with his cane, and once again the little door opened and the coachman craned his neck to look down into the dark interior of the carriage. "I say, driver, this *is* the *twelfth*, is it not?" The tapping noise had startled the horse slightly, it seemed. He jolted toward one side of the road, and there was the sound of a thump.

"Yes, sir, the twelfth of September, sir," the driver said, tightening the reins.

"Thank you," Mr. Self mumbled, now looking confused and uncomfortable.

In a little while, and only two or three minutes past the appointed time, the carriage drew up in front of the beautiful carved doors, which now were standing wide open as people were walking, crawling, and being carried in. He very nearly asked the coachman to take him immediately back to the village, but, rather astonishingly, the coachman himself, after opening the door for Mr. Self to step out of the carriage, turned and entered the big house. What in the world was going on, Mr. Self wondered? What in the world? He stood still, outside the door of the big house, as the oddest assortment of people passed him.

"Come along, dearie," said a woman's voice as an arm took hold of his and drew him forward.

"What, why, who . . . ?" he said, turning and seeing the face of one of those red-lipsticked, heavily perfumed, scandalously dressed women his carriage had passed on the road. He was so stunned that he allowed himself to be pulled along forward through the door, but, once in the great hallway, he came to himself and shook free of the woman's grip with a grunt of disgust. "Really!" he said. She looked back briefly, shrugged, and merged into the flow of the other people surging forward toward what must be the dining hall.

"Good evening, sir," said a familiar voice at his right elbow. Mr. Self turned his head and saw, to his great surprise, his servant, Mr. Hobbs. "So good of you to give me the night off, sir."

Mr. Self stood speechless. Mr. Hobbs took a few steps forward, then halted, and looked back at his employer. "I believe we are expected in the dining room, sir." He waited until Mr. Self re-composed himself, removed his top hat, and placed it, along with his cape, on a coat hook along the wall where others had placed their outer garments. He removed his gloves and stuffed them in the pocket of his cape, and leaned his cane against the wall. There really should have been an attendant to take the guest's things, he thought, then considered the irony that his own servant had apparently been invited into the same dining hall as himself. He cleared his throat and followed in the direction of the crowd, increasing his pace so as to walk a few steps ahead, rather than alongside, Mr. Hobbs.

As they entered the dining hall, each person in turn was greeted at the door by their host himself. Mr. Self was frankly put off by the manner of the owner of the big house, who, rather than shaking the hand of each guest, or bowing, actually embraced each person, and then gestured to a seat at the great wide table. But as he stood in line awaiting his turn to be greeted, Mr. Self's attention was arrested by the very size of the table. Never had he seen anything like it, nor even imagined such a thing. It must have been large enough to seat a hundred people. It filled up the dining hall, which itself was huge. In fact, except for the great hallway through which everyone had entered, the dining hall seemed to take up practically the entire house. And yet, there was an unusual intimacy about the room; large as it was, it was not cavernous, but festive and welcoming.

As it happened, Mr. Hobbs was directly behind Mr. Self in the reception line, and when their host turned his attention from the previous guest, his eyes seemed to fall first on Mr. Hobbs. A great smile broke out on their host's face as he reached out his arms past the expectant Mr. Self and embraced Mr. Hobbs, his servant. "My good friend, Josiah Hobbs. How good of you to come. How wonderful to see you again."

Mr. Self was dumbfounded.

"May I present my employer, Mr. Tobias Self? I'm not sure that you've met."

Mr. Self put out his hand, thinking also that he might bow, but his host ignored the gesture and instead reached out his arms around Mr. Self and embraced him as warmly as a dear old friend. "Thank you so much for coming," said their host. "I believe your places are just over there," he said, pointing to two empty chairs and starting to lead them to the spot.

Mr. Self felt quite uncomfortable sitting next to his servant at a dinner table. For his part, Mr. Hobbs seemed to feel quite at home with the arrangement and made a comment on the fine crystal on the table, to which Mr. Self gave a mumbled assent. He could scarcely believe the assortment of people with whom he was apparently expected to dine. He quite obviously was not at the head of the table. Any thought that the dinner was being held just for his sake had evaporated by now.

Mr. Self and his servant had been just about the last people to be seated. Their host now came round to a place at the opposite side of the massive dining table. "I am so pleased that you could all come and join me for dinner," he said graciously. "I have long looked forward to this feast with you all. Indeed, I have been preparing for it all these many years. So now . . . . Oh, dear."

He had interrupted his remarks just as the door to the kitchen had opened and a gaily dressed young girl stood holding a tray of bowls steaming with what must have been soup, emitting a delicious smell that immediately filled the hall. He was staring at an empty place at the table. "Where's Phoebe Lamb?" he asked. "Did she not come?"

Mr. Self saw that it was the only place at the table that was not occupied.

"Is Miss Lamb not present?"

The red-lipsticked woman who had tried to pull Mr. Self into the big house stood up at her place. "She was with me on the road coming up from the village, but then we got separated. I know that she intended to be here. I know that she wanted to come."

Their host looked most distressed. "Let's get on with it," thought Mr. Self, who was by now rather hungry, and, given the unsavoriness of some of the guests, was really wishing that the evening would be shorter rather than longer.

"We must find her," said their host, much distressed. "There are dangers in the forest. It's getting dark. She may be lost. She may be injured. We can't be partying while she's missing." He hastened toward the hallway and, taking with him an ornamental lamp from a little stand near the front door, he plunged out into the night.

"Really," Mr. Self could not help himself from saying. "This is *most* out of order."

He looked at Mr. Hobbs, whose face showed no sympathy with his employer's sense of disgust, but was all anxiety for the missing guest. Mr. Hobbs suddenly leaped from his chair. "Come on," he shouted. "Everybody! We must find Miss Lamb!"

"Oh, poor Phoebe!" Mr. Self could hear the drone of the red-lipsticked, perfume-reeking woman in the scandalous dress, and he realized in disgust that the tardy dinner guest must have been the *other* red-lipsticked, perfume-reeking woman in the scandalous dress that his carriage had passed on the road.

"Really!" Mr. Self said again, this time with greater emphasis, as he steadfastly remained seated while the rest of the company around him sprung to their feet. He sat alone at the table, becoming aware again of his hunger. Chairs were toppled all around him, a strange silence having descended on the hall. After a few minutes, he pushed back his chair and rose to his feet and made his way to the kitchen door, selected one of the bowls from the tray that had been hastily abandoned upon the news of Phoebe Lamb's absence, and took it back to his place at the table. The soup really was quite good, the best that he could remember.

After what must have been nearly an hour—there was a disturbing lack of clocks in the house—Mr. Self, who had also found and helped himself to a relish tray and some rolls, quite delicious, detected a growing chorus of voices coming from outside the front door of the big house. He heard the door swing open and the voices that mixed laughing with singing grew suddenly louder as the crowd pushed into the dining room. "Halle, halle, hallelujah," they seemed to be singing to some foreign rhythm. He was absolutely shocked to see his host carrying a red-lipsticked, perfume-reeking woman in a scandalous dress seated on his shoulder, like some sort of a hero. He could see that her hair was disheveled and her cheek was bruised.

As they passed where he sat staring at them, his host informed him in a tone that was informational, not condemnatory, "Found her sitting dazed in the trees alongside the lane. Someone's carriage had bumped into her and shoved her off the road, where she fell and no one noticed as they walked by. A good thing we went looking for her. It's beginning to snow." Mr. Self now noticed for the first time that people's shoes were wet, and they had tracked some mud into the dining hall. There were drops of water on their shoulders, and the hair of some people was stringy and damp.

Phoebe Lamb was gently lowered from her host's shoulder by some of her fellow guests. "Well," said their host after everyone had righted their chairs and resumed their places at the huge table, and he had tried to neaten his own hair a bit by running his fingers through it. "Now, we can eat."

Mr. Self, just then, had to stifle a burp.

Twenty-fifth Sunday in Ordinary Time
Spanish Springs Presbyterian Church, Sparks, Nevada
September 23, 2007

Jeremiah 8:18—9:1
1 Timothy 2:1–7
Luke 16:1–13

"Isn't He the God of All?"

The army captain looked up at the young man seated across the flimsy table from him, formulating in his mind how to approach the issue. Angry as he was, still, he had regarded it as unseemly to have a man of the cloth stand at attention in his presence, so he had invited him to sit down as soon as he had entered the tent. The captain did not consider himself to be a religious man. That department, he had left to his wife and children. But he had always tried to treat the subject with respect, *and* its *proponents*, whether they wore a clerical collar or not. He had always felt uneasy around ministers and priests, less so around chaplains, but he never felt like he quite understood them, and that had always bothered him. He prided himself on being able to read a person upon first meeting, especially those under his command. *His* safety, and *theirs*, and the safety of *others*, might *depend* upon it. He himself liked plain-speaking, forthright men, decisive men, men of action. The young man he had summoned to his field headquarters did not seem to answer any of those descriptions. But the situation the young man had created—and, by thunder, *he* was the one who had *created* it—was delicate. Not that the captain cared much what the young man might think about what he had to say, but the effect on his troops and on his stature among them if it came to be known that he had dressed down a man of God—that was something, as a military leader, he had to consider. Other chaplains who had been under his command had seemed more mature, more suited for their role on the battlefield.

"I asked you here," the captain began, "because of some things that you said this morning in the service."

"Yes," the other man said, appearing—what was it?—either nervous or confused, it was unclear.

"You understand, don't you, that the success of this war depends upon soldiers like the ones you were speaking to this morning? Whether we win or lose, whether they live or die on the battlefield, whether their *comrades* live or die?"

"Yes, captain," the other man said again.

"So that what you say, and the effect it has on their morale, has serious consequences, and becomes my concern."

"Yes," the other man said yet again, adding, this time, "I am aware of that."

The captain wished that the conversation could have stopped there, his point made. But the young man seated across the table signaled no remorse, indeed, showed no indication that he understood what the captain was referring to at all. Under the circumstances, the captain was left with no alternative but to be blunt.

"What you said this morning, I believe, *could* and very likely *will* have a damaging effect on this company."

The other man looked surprised and appeared not to appreciate the situation.

"As a military chaplain, it is your responsibility to bolster the morale of these troops. What in the world were you thinking when you asked them to pray for the enemy and that blood-thirsty leader of theirs?"

Now, the other man comprehended the nature of his alleged offense. "Sir, I was preaching a sermon drawn from the teaching of scripture, and I offered a prayer based on it."

"Then I think your choice of 'scripture' was inappropriate, and your prayer was mis-spoken. You are here in the service of the military, and the job of the military is to fight the enemy and prevail, not to welcome him into your Sunday school class."

The other man blanched somewhat at this last comment. He recognized his relative youth and inexperience. He had never expected to find himself on the front lines of battle, but, when he graduated from seminary, there were no church positions immediately available, and he had been persuaded to become a military chaplain, supposing he would be posted on a permanent military base somewhere. His training for the role, emphasizing solace for the wounded and the bereaved, had been brief, owing to the critical shortage of chaplains and the urgent need to post them, and he had found himself ministering to troops in the field.

"I find nothing in the Bible," he responded after a few seconds' pause, "to suggest that Christ regards our enemies as any less in need of our prayers than our friends are."

"Prayers for their *health*, and that they will not suffer *harm*? What the h . . . , what in the world do you think war is *about*, Lieutenant?"

The chaplain was not accustomed to being addressed by his military rank. "It is about human failure, sir. It is about human sin."

This angered the captain, but the officer was beginning to feel out of his depth. He decided to focus his comments on the welfare of his own troops rather than tread the unfamiliar and bewildering territory of theology. "Morale, Lieutenant, morale. How are these men going to feel about killing someone they've just *prayed* for? If these men aren't willing to kill the *enemy*, even if *you* happen to regard that as a *sin*, *they're* going to *die*. Is *that* what you want? Is that what *God* wants? Is that what the *Bible* says to do?"

"The Bible," the chaplain said, clearing his throat and sitting up a little more stiffly, "says, in the portion I read and preached about this morning, to give supplications, prayers, intercessions, and thanksgiving for *all* people, for kings and for all who are in high positions. I hear, in that teaching, no exceptions. It is easy and natural for us to pray for those who do us good. The *Christian* is supposed to go *further*. I was merely preaching today what the Bible says, and praying in the way that the Bible says to pray. And nowhere in the teachings of our Lord do I find a command to work the destruction of one's enemies, but to *love* them, and, even, to *pray* for them, as *I* would wish to be prayed for."

Under his combat uniform, the captain was simmering, wishing that he had not gotten into an attitude of discussion but had simply stated his objection and perhaps requested that the young chaplain be relieved of his post. Other, older chaplains he had dealt with had wiser approaches to their role on the battlefield, seemed to understand much better their function in the overall strategy for victory.

"So, you would pray for the well-being of our enemy. And how is that not treason, mister?"

"By 'treason,' do you mean disloyalty to God, sir?"

"Don't play games with me, Lieutenant. Aiding and comforting the enemy is a serious matter. Invoking the Almighty to protect the enemy is, shall we say, counter-productive." He leaned back in his chair and stroked his moustache. "Tell me, do you think that God really wants these butchers to win? You've seen their atrocities. You've heard the ravings of that maniac president of theirs. What God worth his title would want them to win?"

"On the basis of what Jesus said, I think it's unlikely that God wants *either* side to *win* so much as he wants the *war* to *end*. But I wasn't preaching in favor of *their victory* or *our loss*, or *praying* for *either* of those outcomes. If that is what you think I said, you greatly misunderstood me."

"That's what your congregation heard, I can assure you."

"Has any of the men said so?" the chaplain inquired.

"You are bordering on insubordination, mister."

"I will follow your orders, sir, as I have done since my posting here, insofar as they do not contradict my commission to preach the gospel and minister according to the tenets of the faith." After a brief pause, he added, "That's what I was doing this morning."

"And your God doesn't want us to win this war?"

"There is but one true God. And that one is the God of *all*—the God of the men, women, and children on the *other* side of the battle lines as surely as he is *our* God. Has there ever been a war in which both sides were not convinced that God was on *their* side, that God supported *their* cause?"

The captain looked exasperated.

"I had an old-fashioned teacher in junior high school," the chaplain said.

The captain sighed and rolled his eyes. But the chaplain continued.

"She made us choose a famous speech and memorize it and recite it to the class. I chose President Lincoln's second inaugural address. Do you remember it, sir?"

The captain responded caustically, "I didn't attend that school."

"I'm sure you've heard parts of it," the chaplain said, ignoring the sarcasm. "Abraham Lincoln, just weeks before he was killed and as the Civil War was continuing, said"—and here, he closed his eyes in an effort to remember correctly—"'Neither party expected for the war the magnitude or the duration which it has already attained. Neither anticipated that the *cause* of the conflict might cease *with* or even *before* the conflict *itself* should cease. Each looked for an easier triumph, and a result less fundamental and astounding.'" At this point, the young man paused briefly for emphasis, and then continued. "'Both read the same Bible and pray to the same God, and each invokes His aid against the other. It may seem strange that any men should dare to ask a just God's assistance in wringing their bread from the sweat of other men's faces, but let us judge not, that we be not judged. The prayers of both could not be answered. That of neither has been answered fully. The Almighty has His own purposes.'" He opened his eyes and looked at the captain. Then he said. "No one can claim to know God's mind. But none of us has the prerogative of closing our heart to another. 'With malice toward none, with charity for all, with firmness in the right as God gives us to see the right, let us strive on to finish the work we are in, to bind up the nation's wounds, to care for him who shall have borne the battle and for his widow and his orphan, to do all which may achieve and cherish a just and lasting peace among ourselves and with all nations.'"[1]

The chaplain reached into his breast pocket and pulled out a small black book, thumbed its thin pages to a particular place, and read, slowly and deliberately, "'*First* of all, then, I urge that supplications, prayers, intercessions, and thanksgivings be made for *everyone*, for kings and all who are in high positions, so that we may lead a quiet and peaceable life in all godliness and dignity. This is right and is acceptable in the sight of God our Savior, who desires *everyone* to be saved and to come to the knowledge of the truth. For there is *one* God; there is also one mediator between God and humankind, Christ Jesus, himself human, who gave himself a ransom for *all*'" (1 Tim 1:6a). He turned back several pages and, finding the spot that he was seeking, again began to read. "''But I say to you that listen, Love your enemies, do good to those who hate you, bless those who curse you, pray for those who abuse you. . . . Do to others as you would have them do to you. If you love those who love you, what credit is that to you? For even sinners love those who love them. If you do good to those who do good to you, what credit is that to you? For even sinners do the same. . . . But love your enemies, do good . . . . Your reward will be great, and you will be children of the Most High; for he is kind to the ungrateful and the wicked. Be merciful, just as your Father is merciful'''" (Luke 6:27, 31–33, 35–36). He closed the book slowly, meditatively, and returned it to his pocket. "I believe, sir, I was doing my duty. Or, that's what I was trying to do. And that is what I must continue to do. It is certainly not my intention to undermine morale. It is my obligation, though, to preach the Word and pray as the Bible directs."

The captain grunted, but it was unclear whether he did so from exasperation or resignation. Eventually, he said, now without any trace of hostility in his voice, "As long as there are wars, you have to want to kill your enemy."

The chaplain replied, "As long as you want to kill your enemy, there will be wars." After a pause, he added, "As you suggested yourself a few minutes ago, sir, how can you kill someone that you've just prayed for?"

The two men fell silent, looking at each other, but their postures now relaxed and their faces thoughtful. They had both entered into a realm of truth-seeking in which there are no combatants, only companions—no divisive contest, only a mutual goal. There was no sound, except for the occasional ripple of a light breeze upon the canvas of the captain's tent. "I

---

1. National Park Service, "Lincoln's Second Inaugural Address."

could request to have you transferred," the captain said, finally, but without any anger in his statement.

"But that really wouldn't solve the issue, would it, sir?"

There was more silence. But it was suddenly broken by a flurry of activity outside the tent, and a sergeant burst in upon them. He gave a quick salute and blurted out the words like a machine gun, "Excuse me, sir. Incoming mortar fire."

"Alert the men," said the captain to the sergeant as both he and the chaplain rose from their chairs.

"Permission to return to duty?" asked the chaplain, turning to leave.

"Granted," the captain said, and the chaplain immediately disappeared through the flaps of the tent. The captain quickly donned his flak jacket and helmet and reached for his binoculars. And, as he reached the entrance of the tent, he said, "God, keep us safe." After a brief pause, he added, "And them."

Twenty-sixth Sunday in Ordinary Time
Lutheran Church of the Master, Lakewood, Colorado
September 25, 2022

Amos 6:1a, 4–7
1 Timothy 6:6–19
Luke 16:19–31

"Who's Lying at Our Gate?"

One of the most important reasons for using the lectionary—a list of Old Testament, Psalm, epistle, and Gospel readings for each Sunday—is that it directs us into parts of the Bible that we might otherwise be quite happy to *ignore*. In doing so, it challenges preachers to be *prophetic*—to pronounce God's *judgment* as well as voicing God's *promise*. It helps congregations to hear the *whole* word of God—to attend to the full sweep of God's purpose, so that we don't pick our *favorite parts* and miss the *entirety*. Some Sundays, the lectionary directs us to readings that make everybody squirm a bit. Some Sundays, the lectionary directs us to readings that give some of us great comfort and hope while distressing and even offending others. Sometimes, the focus is on individual behaviors or attitudes. Sometimes, whole cultures and ways of life are addressed. The task of the preacher and the congregation, of course, is not to speak and hear things that are *popular*, but to advocate and do the things that are *faithful*.

    I suspect that there are some churches in which today's passages from First Timothy and the Gospel of Luke are never read, or at least are seldom preached upon. For much of my career, I was a new church development pastor, and I am aware that there are schools of church growth that recommend avoiding some parts of the Bible on the grounds that they might "turn off" or upset prospective members. And I know that there are some churches that are so wrapped up in the ideals and goals of the culture, and of its political and economic systems, that the plain meaning of today's scripture passages, if these passages are mentioned at all, is distorted into some message like "Jesus wants you to be *wealthy*," or "Jesus wants you to *stay* wealthy." There was a very practical reason that the medieval clergy and the medieval nobility were allied in trying to keep the scriptures out of the hands of the common people. There was a very practical reason that Southern slave owners discouraged teaching black folk to read. What would happen if people came to realize that there were passages like these in the Bible—passages that declare God's great concern for the poor and God's terrible judgment upon the rich?

Of course, *all* Bible passages should be read in context. So, let us back up a few verses to notice that the parable that Jesus told about a rich man, whose name we aren't given, and a poor man, whose name was Lazarus, was Jesus' response to being ridiculed by some Pharisees, whom Luke informs us "were lovers of money" (Luke 16:14). "So [Jesus] said to them, 'You are those who justify yourselves in the sight of others; but God knows your hearts; for what is prized by human beings is an abomination in the sight of God'" (16:15). And a few verses later, Jesus told the story about a rich man who was dressed in opulent garments and ate lavish meals every day, and about a poor man who lay at the doorstep of the rich man's house—presumably, a crippled beggar.

The poor man—Lazarus—"longed to satisfy his hunger with what fell from the rich man's table" (16:21a). In those days, at a feast, the diners would use chunks of bread to wipe the grease off their hands, and then simply throw the bread on the floor. Lazarus would have welcomed even such messy—may we say "gross"?—discards. But the rich man never gave him any heed in life—even, it seems, if he had to step over him whenever he went in and out of his house. Not only was Lazarus hungry, he was covered with sores. And we mustn't suppose that the dogs were licking him out of affection. The ancient Jews considered dogs to be unclean; the scene Jesus painted was supposed to be disgusting, not endearing. The rich man, so conspicuous in his consumption, even had a gate to separate himself from the riffraff of the city—those who were hungry, those who were sick, those who were poor. Finally, Lazarus died of starvation and disease at the rich man's gate, just a few feet away from a sumptuous table laden with food. One wonders what Jesus would have made of "gated communities."

What direct hand the rich man might have played in *creating* Lazarus' poverty or *causing* his illness, we don't know. Perhaps none. What we *do* know is that he took no hand in *helping* him. Clearly, the condition of Lazarus did not prompt the rich man to change anything about his own life. The popular view was that someone like Lazarus really wasn't worth anybody's time or concern; obviously, God had abandoned him—to be in such a wretched condition, popular opinion held, he *must* have been a *sinner*, it *must* have been his own *fault*. In neglecting Lazarus, the rich man would not have been considered "bad" by his friends or by society at large. He was breaking no civil law. And he was not a criminal. But he *was* ignoring the law of *God* which shouts from one end of the Bible to the other about how to treat our neighbor, including especially the poor and the suffering and the unattractive.

In my childhood, my family lived on the western slopes of Mount Franklin in El Paso. Along the Rio Grande, just north of downtown El Paso and just below the University of Texas at El Paso, is the site of what in those days was one of the largest smelters in the world, where huge amounts of raw ore were processed daily and gold and silver and other metals were extracted and refined. From our backyard up on the mountainside above, we could see the glow every evening from the dross—the red-hot slag being poured out in mounds at the end of the day. Closer to the smelter, it would illuminate the surroundings with an orange light and cast eerie shadows. Gold and silver—the age-old symbols of wealth. But just a few hundred yards down and across the river in Mexico was one of the poorest spots in North America—a vast squatters' village of shanties, some made of nothing more sturdy than cardboard. In the dust of summertime, it probably felt good for the kids to go barefoot, as they did; shoes were a luxury. But in the muck and mire caused by the fall monsoons, it was a different story, and in the snows that occasionally fell in the wintertime. There were beggars among them, who would come into downtown Juarez and hold their hands out to the tourists. And there were "wetbacks," as they were derisively called, who crossed the river and illegally climbed over fences or slipped under them just to try to find day labor in El Paso, in the simple belief that *everyone* is entitled to *eat*. The best they could hope for would be to become permanent members of the servant class. After a while, you tended not to see the squatters' settlement, or not to see it for what it was. It became just a part of the landscape to us who were able to eat three good meals a day. You lost perspective on whether it was a tragedy or a nuisance. "How can people live like that?" you sometimes heard people ask each other, even in between bites of dinner.

The day came when, overtaken by his sores and his crippling disease, or perhaps by his hunger, Lazarus died. Having been neglected by others in his earthly life, Lazarus was prized nevertheless in the eyes of God, who sent his angels to bring him to Abraham's side. The rich man also died—was it of clogged arteries?—but found himself (surprise!) not in a place of honor and privilege, but in torment in the flames of hell. He looked up and saw

Abraham, and recognized also the beggar who had lain at his gate all those long years. "'Father Abraham,'" he said, "'have mercy on me, and send Lazarus to dip the tip of his finger in water and cool my tongue; for I am in agony in these flames'" (16:24). But the man who had taken no pity on a neighbor who was in agony during *his* life would receive nothing now that *he himself* was in agony. Abraham informed him that the situation of the rich and the poor had been reversed; the gate that he might have opened up to Lazarus to give him a meal and bandage his wounds had now been replaced by a large chasm that no one could cross, not even to give a drop of water. It was of no avail that the rich man was a child of Abraham—a person publicly regarded as one of God's own, his status confirmed in popular opinion by his riches. Not even his religious pedigree could bring the wealthy man the slightest relief in death when he had so ignored the needs of the poor in life. While he was *in* the world, he had put his trust in his bank account and his pantry—the things *of* the world; where was his solace now that he had been *removed* from the world? He had neglected his *neighbor* in *life*; why should his *neighbor* remember *him* in *death*? Still thinking of Lazarus as nothing more to him than a potential errand boy, the rich man said, "'Then, father [Abraham], I beg you to send [Lazarus] to my father's house—for I have five brothers—that he may warn them, so that *they* will not also come into this place of torment.' Abraham replied, 'They have Moses and the prophets; they should listen to them'" (16:27-29). All they had to do, Abraham was saying, is read the Bible—it tells over and over again about God's concern for the poor. It plainly states that the duty of individuals, and their rulers, is to feed the hungry and house the homeless and care for the sick and welcome the stranger. "'No, father Abraham; but if someone goes to them from the dead, they will repent'" (16:30). Abraham said to him, "'If they do not listen to Moses and the prophets, neither will they be convinced even if someone rises from the dead'" (16:31).

The resurrection of Jesus hasn't even convinced all *Christians* to have compassion for the poor. I've heard some Christians even claim that it is their virtuous duty *not* to help the poor. It would just make them lazy. It would make them dependent. "God helps those who help themselves." (By the way, that's not in the Bible.) Two chapters after the parable of the rich man and Lazarus, Jesus answers a ruler's question what he must do to inherit eternal life; already, he kept the Ten Commandments. "'There is still one thing lacking,'" said Jesus. "'Sell all that you own and distribute the money to the poor'" (18:22). Are we wiser than Jesus? If we somehow think that giving to the poor to our own material disadvantage, or restructuring society to eliminate poverty at the cost of our own affluence, would have a damaging effect on the poor person's spiritual life, perhaps we need to consider the effect on *our* spiritual life if we do *not* do so: "Those who want to be rich fall into temptation and are trapped by many senseless and harmful desires that plunge people into ruin and destruction," says First Timothy. "For the love of money is a root of all kinds of evil, and in their eagerness to be rich some have wandered away from the faith" (1 Tim 6:9–10). And you and I, friends, are rich beyond the dreaming of those who dwell in the shantytowns of the world, rich beyond the imagining of a lot of people right here in metro Denver. By the way, the smelter is closed now, and the company, as a condition of one of the largest environmental bankruptcies in history, has had to pay fifty-two million dollars to try to clean up the mess created by all that refining of gold and silver, which doesn't even take into account the effects on the health of the people who lived near the smelter, including so many who were so very poor. Such is the legacy sometimes left by the pursuit of great wealth.

But ultimately, the rich man's sin wasn't his gluttony and his disregard of the poor. His sin was the fact that he put his trust in the things of the *world* rather than putting his confidence in *God*. So his situation after *death* was just the *consequence* of the way he had lived his *life*. It would have taken more than dropping a few coins at Lazarus' feet to alter the outcome here. He didn't need to give just the spare change in his pocket; he needed to change his whole attitude and his whole way of life. It meant being content to live with *less* so that others could have *enough*. And *that* would mean a fundamental shift in values away from *acquiring* and *possessing* to *giving* and *sharing*. Any material thing that we have in life is more than we *entered* life with, and more than we will be able to *leave* life with. God told the chosen people long ago in Sinai that they were to be content with what came to them from God's hand to sustain them day by day, and not to store it up; they were supposed to learn to trust God's provision, and to guarantee that everyone had enough—even the weakest, the sickest, the least skilled and the least intelligent. Today, while a quarter of the earth's population is malnourished or starving, enough food is produced in the world for every man, woman, and child to eat well. And while a lot of us think that we absolutely must have a faster computer modem, millions are desperate for just a few more grains of rice. The problem is much more profound than flinging a few coins at a beggar and donating our discards and leftovers, like crumbs from the table. It requires a radical solution. It may even mean that you and I and all of us together will have to change, so that we *see* and truly *care for* those who are lying at *our* gate.

Twenty-seventh Sunday in Ordinary Time

Spanish Springs Presbyterian Church, Sparks, Nevada

October 7, 2007

Lamentations 1:1–6
2 Timothy 1:1–14
Luke 17:5–10

"From Generation to Generation"

We live in an age that assumes everything worthwhile must be programmed, scheduled, planned. It begins in young childhood, in fact even before the baby is born. In some parts of the country, and, I assume, in some areas of Reno and Sparks, anxious parents-to-be get their names on waiting lists for the best preschool openings. They want every intellectual advantage for their child from the very beginning of life. Some babies are subjected to hearing a precise amount of Mozart each day, some to a precise amount of the *Wall Street Journal*, depending upon whether the parents hope for a musical virtuoso or a business magnate. Little children are enrolled in ballet or barely-out-of-diapers football. Even children's play time has taken on the terminology of a business appointment and is planned for its developmental potential—we hear references to "play dates." Childhood is being structured for success, and the better toys are the ones that don't simply *amuse*. But our culture's definition of "success" seems to take little account of what is most important in life: relationships—relationships with one another, relationships with God. Oh, there is plenty of attention given to how to *manipulate* other people, how to get out of them something that we *want*. But all of the scheduling for success leaves very little room for what the Christian faith, and the Bible, claim to be the most important aspect of life.

A news report a couple of weeks ago cited a study that confirmed what a lot of parents over many centuries have known intuitively. It is the children of families that make a point of eating dinner together that are least likely to get into trouble, meaning, these days (in terms of the study), drinking, smoking, drugs, and the like. The television report did not go into further detail, but I suspect that there might well be some correlation, too, with how well children do in school and how well children do in relationships. It isn't just an issue of *where* or *when* a person eats, of course. It isn't just a matter of sharing *food*, but of sharing *life*—showing an interest in and learning about and contributing to what the family members are doing and experiencing in school, at the workplace, at leisure, and what they are thinking about, and what they value. It would surely be oversimplifying to propose a direct link between the increase in gang violence and the decline of the ritual of the family dinner in contemporary America, but there is at least an *indirect* link between the disappearance of the daily gathering of the household around the dinner table and the increase in the fragmentation and dysfunction of the family and society at large.

The Bible knows its own many examples of dysfunctional families. Most of the main characters of the Old Testament came from them. But in the New Testament, there is an intriguing suggestion that one family functioned pretty well. Many scholars think that the letters to Timothy were most likely circular letters of instruction written to be *passed between* and *read by* several different churches in Asia. The style and the vocabulary are very different from those of the letters that we are certain Paul wrote himself to specific churches or individuals, and that fact casts doubt that First and Second Timothy were actually written by Paul. But then there are those remarkably personal references, such as Paul might have made when writing to his young protégé, chief among them that very appealing verse, "I am reminded of your sincere faith, a faith that lived first in your grandmother Lois and your mother Eunice and now, I am sure, lives in you" (2 Tim 1:5).

Timothy was the child of a mixed marriage. His mother was a Jewish Christian, but his father was Greek, apparently a non-believer. His home was at Lystra in the Roman province of Galatia, in which Paul had been active as a missionary, preaching the faith and establishing churches. Paul had come to Lystra on his first missionary journey. It was probably then that Paul first met Timothy. When Paul *returned* to Lystra, he had found that Timothy had grown to Christian maturity, and he decided to invite him to come along as a fellow worker in the mission field. The local church leaders formally commissioned the young man and gave him their blessing, and from then on he traveled with Paul and frequently served as his envoy. Several of Paul's letters indicate that Timothy was with him when they were written, and he is cited as joining Paul in sending greetings to those various Christian congregations Paul addresses. As we have them, First and Second

Timothy are addressed as if sent to Timothy while he was working in Ephesus, battling dangerous heresies and threatened by persecution while dealing with other issues that even today are regularly a part of what ministers and congregations face.

"A faith that lived first in your grandmother Lois and your mother Eunice and now, I am sure, lives in you" (2 Tim 1:5). This afternoon, we will begin the most recent of our new member and inquirer classes. In the first session of each class, we take some time to think about the people and events that have influenced our faith. Participants in the class will sometimes mention a church school teacher, sometimes even a minister. But most often, people will refer to a parent or a grandparent as a person who, by precept or by example, most influenced them in their Christian development. And, it seems to me, as I think back over the scores of new member and inquirer classes I have taught in four different churches now, that the people who did *not* have that constant Christian nurture at home felt deeply the loss and disadvantage. In no case that I can remember was it an instance of the parent or grandparent sitting the person down for *formal* instruction. It was more in the way of taking them with them to worship, seeing that they were in church school and youth group, reading the Bible with them and praying with them at home, and providing an example in their actions and their conversation, often at the dinner table.

Jesus frequently taught at the table. Especially in Luke, which refers to more meals than any of the other Gospels, we see that Jesus used mealtimes as occasions for communicating the things of God. Sometimes, the meal *itself* became an object lesson, as for instance the episode of which we read a few weeks ago, when Jesus commented on the order in which people were seating themselves at a banquet, and of course there is the Last Supper, during which Jesus interpreted the events of the next day, Good Friday, in terms of what the disciples were eating and drinking. It would have been the most natural thing in the household of Lois and Eunice for there to have been discussion at the family table about Christ, and for these women to have shown in their domestic activities and manners how their faith in Christ had a fundamental influence on their lives. They had no New Testament to read to young Timothy at that point, but they knew the scriptures of what became the *Old* Testament, and they believed that Jesus was the fulfillment of all that had been established by God in the law and promised by God through the prophets. They were very likely the earliest examples in Timothy's life of the power and the love and the self-discipline spoken of in this morning's reading, and theirs were very likely the hands that, metaphorically speaking, laid the kindling to which the Holy Spirit was able to spark the flame of faith in the boy. It might have been the great apostle Paul who *brought* the gospel to places like Ephesus and Corinth and Thessalonica, but it was associates like Timothy, faithfully and patiently *nurturing* the churches in those places, who deserve much of the credit for the *spread* of Christianity throughout Asia Minor and Europe. And that means that it was countless parents and grandparents like Eunice and Lois, and other Christian relatives and friends, for whom we should also give thanks to God.

In my own case, I credit my parents and my grandmothers for my Christian upbringing, and an elderly babysitting couple in Salt Lake City, and church school and vacation church school teachers in El Paso, and my mother's cousin (my second cousin) who was a teacher in the public school in her small town in northwestern Kansas and who was also a Christian educator for the Western Kansas district of the United Methodist Church. Beulah, among other things, was an excellent cook, and whenever we were in Bird City, Kansas (which oftentimes was for Thanksgiving dinner), there was a lot of activity in her kitchen and around her table. The meals were always relaxed with lots of conversation—catching up, looking forward, learning about what each person at the table was doing and was interested in, always positive, always gently encouraging, always with much laughter, and always involving issues of faith in a most natural way. Beulah's husband Kenneth, who sat at the head of the table and was the local postmaster, epitomized the pace of life in Bird City—never rushed—and he un-self-consciously helped establish the principle that, while the *food* was the *occasion* for *gathering* at the table, something a lot more *important* than just *eating* was *happening* there. The table was the place where generations met and the most important business of life was transacted, and the transaction of that business had little to do with stock prices or commodities, was not determined by international affairs or political machinations, went on despite the claims of society and culture that there were more important things to be doing, more productive ways to spend our time, more efficient ways to convey data.

For many centuries, it has been so—the principal place that the faith has been passed on from generation to generation, as it must have been from Lois to Eunice to Timothy, has been at the *table*, not just in the *eating* but also in the very acts of gathering, remembering, encouraging, rejoicing, rekindling and conveying the family tradition of faith.

> Paul, an apostle of Christ Jesus by the will of God, for the sake of the promise of life that is in Christ Jesus, To Timothy, my beloved child: Grace, mercy, and peace from God the Father and Christ Jesus our Lord. I am grateful to God—whom I worship with a clear conscience, as my *ancestors* did—when I

> remember you constantly in my prayers night and day. Recalling your tears, I long to see you so that I may be filled with joy. I am reminded of your sincere faith, a faith that lived first in your grandmother Lois and your mother Eunice and now, I am sure, lives in you. (2 Tim 1:1–5)

Parents, never underestimate the influence you have over your children, and the memories they will have of what was discussed at the family table, and what was modeled there. Grandparents, never underestimate the influence you have over your grandchildren, and how, in those times of eating together with you, they learned the values and wisdom that characterize Christian maturity. Grandparents, parents, children—it's almost mealtime now, time to take your place at the table.

Twenty-eighth Sunday in Ordinary Time
Spanish Springs Presbyterian Church, Sparks, Nevada
October 10, 2010

Jeremiah 29:1, 4–7
2 Timothy 2:8–15
Luke 17:11–19

"A Blessing to the Nations"

Luke the evangelist, most Bible scholars agree, was not a Jew. He was probably a Greek, one of the many converts made by the apostle Paul to the gospel of Jesus Christ, the crucified and risen Son of the God whom Israel worshiped. In Luke's day, a residue of suspicion still formed something of a wall between Christians of *Jewish* background—those who still considered it necessary to follow all of the laws of Moses, including the laws about circumcision and what the faithful may and may not eat—and Christians of *Gentile* background—Greeks and others attracted to Christianity by the story of the resurrection and the promise of forgiveness of sins. It is in Luke's Gospel that we find parables in which foreigners feature prominently, including the parable of the Good Samaritan, in which Jesus spoke of the remarkable neighborliness that a person despised by the Jews of his own day showed toward a Judean who had been beaten by ruffians and neglected by his fellow Judeans as they passed by his bruised and bloodied body. It is also in Luke's Gospel that we find stories that highlight the eager belief of *foreigners* in Jesus even while the children of *Abraham* remained *hostile* to Christ.

One of those stories, unique to Luke's Gospel, is about ten men who had leprosy, who called upon Jesus in unison, asking the famed healer to cure them of their disease. Jesus was on his way to Jerusalem, passing through the region along the border between Samaria and Galilee. The lepers were properly observing the rules about keeping their distance from healthy people. So, rather than touch them, as Jesus often did with the sick, he merely told them to go to Jerusalem and show themselves to the priest at the temple so that he could verify they had been cured, as the law required before they could return to society. At the moment they appealed to Jesus, they were still afflicted with their disease. But, having had faith enough in Jesus' power to cure to come seek him out, they now obediently did as Jesus directed, as if indeed they were *already* cured, and, as they went along toward Jerusalem and the temple, they perceived that their leprosy was disappearing. Can you imagine their joy and relief? No longer were they afflicted with pain and unsightliness and deformity, but they could once again enjoy the company of friends and family, could once again approach and be approached, embrace and be embraced, live in society and not be banished to the wilderness camps where lepers were forced to exist until death finally ended their misery.

One of the ten actually disobeyed Jesus; when he saw that he was well, he couldn't resist returning to the man who had healed him. Instead of going straight to the priest as Jesus had directed, this man "turned back, praising God with a loud voice. He prostrated himself at Jesus' feet and thanked him. And he was a Samaritan"—the *one*, among the *ten*, whom Jews would have regarded as a heretic and not worthy of Jesus' notice. "Then Jesus asked, 'Were not *ten* made clean? But the *other* nine, where are *they*? Was none of them found to return and give praise to God except this *foreigner*?'" (Luke 17:15b–18). Yes, the other nine had obeyed Jesus, presumably, by continuing on to see the priest and receive their certificates of good health. Jesus might not have thought anything about it, had the *one* man not *returned*, and *him* the *least* likely, in the popular mind, to *deserve* healing or to praise *God* for it. But he *had* returned, this non-Jew, this child of Abraham who had no background in the prophets and their promise of a Messiah who would come to bring salvation and open the gates of the kingdom of heaven. "Then [Jesus] said to [the Samaritan], 'Get up and go on your way; your faith has made you well'" (17:19). The Greek words could also be translated "Your faith has saved you."

The story, on its face, can be read as simply another episode demonstrating Jesus' power to heal, or to make a point, tinged with anti-Semitism, about the Jews' failure to perceive that Jesus was the Son of God. But Luke would not have bothered to tell us that the grateful man was a Samaritan— maybe wouldn't have included the story in his Gospel at all—unless he considered the man's being a foreigner important, and unless he thought that *Jesus* had considered it important. As a disciple of Paul, who had been so instrumental in carrying the gospel to the Greeks and who had suffered the criticism of his fellow apostles for having done so, Luke *did* have a point to make, and one whose ramifications are still being disregarded by some believers today: the gospel was not intended for the *few*, but for the *many*; salvation is not just for *some*, but for *all*; and the church of Jesus Christ is not to be a *club* with a policy of *exclusion*, but a *fellowship* of *welcome* and *mercy*, the fulfillment of God's promise to Abraham long centuries ago, from whom Jesus was descended, that through Abraham and his offspring, *all* the nations would be blessed. The church was not to be the *end* of God's saving work, but a renewed *beginning*. The church was to be the channel through which God's blessings of forgiveness and redemption would be bestowed broadly and liberally, including upon the very nations that seemed to stand over against Israel and her God. It was ironic that it was *Jewish* leaders, *Israelites*, who had rejected Jesus, had indicted him and convicted him, had arranged for him to be put to death. But that very antagonism had proved the opportunity of God's grace, in its fullness, to flow *outward* from Judea into all the earth.

That is the nature of the grace of God. But, throughout history, many people who profess faith in God have erected barriers to the free flow of God's grace, either intentionally or unintentionally. Some people, preferring to fill up hell rather than fling open the gates of heaven, have denied altogether the notion that God's love is to be shown farther and farther, knocking down the walls of prejudice and hatred and suspicion. When that tendency becomes bound up with nationalistic or racial or ethnic pride and animosity, it is an especially difficult corruption of the faith to counter, for some will start accusing others of being unpatriotic or of being ignorant of the laws of nature or of forgetting their proper allegiances. And, for many people, it flies in the face of the whole notion of some being "elect," which they interpret to mean "elite," "privileged," those few who alone are worthy *of* and destined *for* salvation.

For some reason, America has a long history of being suspicious of foreigners, has often treated immigrants shamefully, despite the fact that the only people who didn't come here from foreign lands are the native Americans. Immigrant group after immigrant group arrived over the centuries, and, as the eighteenth gave way to the nineteenth, and the nineteenth gave way to the twentieth, and now the twentieth has given way to the twenty-first, new arrivals have continued to be met with suspicion, even hostility, and a demand that they show themselves worthy of staking claim on the American dream. It makes no difference that many of them worship the same God, follow the same Christ, believe in the same Holy Spirit, that you and I do—that we are brothers and sisters in the Christian faith. The Old Testament has a lot to say about God's command to accept the foreigner with respect and deal with the alien fairly, to welcome the newcomer and treat him or her as you would a native son or daughter. The *New* Testament signals that God's people can even learn a thing or two about faithfulness and obedience and gratitude to God from someone who has long been considered an outsider.

And what if the tables were reversed? What is the duty of a person of God who finds him- or herself in a foreign land, even one in which God's name is not known and the population worships pagan idols? In one very extraordinary chapter, Jeremiah the prophet delivered the commandment of God to the exiles who had been taken against their will into captivity in Babylon. In this hard case, God's directions were not to try to escape back to the promised land, were not to denounce the Babylonian captors and their idolatrous religion or even to protest their captivity with hunger strikes and refusal to cooperate, but just the opposite. "Build houses and live in them; plant gardens and eat what they produce. Take wives and have sons and daughters; take wives for your sons, and give your daughters in marriage, that *they* may bear sons and daughters; multiply there, and do not decrease" (Jer 29:5–6). Indeed, Jeremiah delivered God's further word that they were to resist any prophets or diviners among the *Israelites* who advised them otherwise or suggested that their time in Babylon was going to be so short that making a home there and settling in for the long haul was pointless or faithless or treasonous. "For thus says the LORD: Only when Babylon's seventy years are completed will I visit you, and I will fulfill to you my promise and bring you back to this place" (29:11). Only after the length of a *lifetime* would they be released back to Judah, meaning that none of the individuals who were taken *into* exile would live to return to their homes in Israel. Their captivity was God's punishment and it was intended to be bitter. Still, it would not crush God's people. But neither would those who had been a part of the faithless generation have the pleasure of seeing Jerusalem again. The future was sure and full of hope, based on God's own plans for their welfare and not for their harm. "Then when you call upon me and come and pray to me, I will hear you. When you search for me, you will find me; if you seek me with all your heart, I will let you find me, says the LORD, and I will restore your fortunes and gather you from all the nations and all the places where I have driven you, says the LORD, and I will bring you back to the place from which I sent you into exile" (29:12–14). But in the meantime—and here is the really remarkable part—"seek the *welfare* of the city where I have sent you into exile, and pray to the LORD on its behalf, for in *its* welfare you will find *your* welfare" (29:7).

From one standpoint, that commandment spoke pragmatically to the Judeans' own self-interest—a plague upon Babylon would sicken the captive Jews as well; a famine upon Babylon would leave the captive Jews hungry as well; a military attack upon Babylon would endanger the captive Jews with injury and death as well. *Their* welfare was now all tied up with the welfare of their *enemy*. But at another level (and we are in a better position to appreciate this today, with our photographs of Earth from space, with our understanding of ecological and economic interdependence, and with Jesus' command to love our enemy and do our enemy good and not harm), it was a matter of *faithfulness*—faithfulness to the God who created the world and every living creature and called them good, faithfulness to the God who will not be confined to national boundaries or ethnic or racial cliques or even to religious creeds, faithfulness to the God who sent his own Son into the world not to condemn but to save and whose *very own countrymen* and *-women* set themselves against him and brought about his death. Could it be that even in the midst of hardship and oppression, and perhaps *through* the hardship and oppression, God's people were going to constitute a blessing to others as Abraham had been promised? "Seek the welfare of the city where I have sent you into exile, and pray to the Lord on its behalf" (29:7)—*not* that it be *destroyed*, *not* that it be *punished* for having besieged Jerusalem and razed the temple and carried her leading citizens into exile, but that it be *blessed* with peace and prosperity and deliverance from every threat and danger.

What a remarkable commandment! But it was also a lesson that being faithful to the God of Israel didn't depend upon being a resident in the land of Palestine any more than it required the existence of the temple or offering up sacrifices there. And it certainly didn't require considering oneself an enemy of foreigners or their religion. In fact, faithfulness required praying for God to cast his mantle of unqualified love and unconditional care over even a pagan land. Being faithful to God meant being a blessing to others, even total *strangers*, even sworn *enemies*, who, having received the benefits of God's grace, may, after all, like the one leper who returned to give thanks, and *he* a *Samaritan*, come to praise God.

Twenty-ninth Sunday in Ordinary Time
Spanish Springs Presbyterian Church, Sparks, Nevada
October 21, 2001

Jeremiah 31:27–34
2 Timothy 3:14—4:5
Luke 18:1–8

"The Other Side of Judgment"

Of all the wonderful experiences that I have had as a parent, from watching first *steps* to hearing first *words*, from admiring first *drawings* to observing first *friendships*, I think what has perhaps thrilled me the most was the first time that each of our children said, "Thank you, Daddy." What the occasions were, I don't recall, but I *do* remember each of their little voices expressing gratitude—*real* gratitude, not just mimicking grown-up words—for a gift, for a meal, for help in getting dressed or assembling a toy. "Thank you, Daddy," meant more than just satisfaction for a desire fulfilled, for some particular deed or present. It meant that Christy, Jesse, and Beth, in turn, had internalized something that is important to their mother and me—to feel and express thanksgiving to the giver, to the doer, to the other person who made some little sacrifice, some little offering of themselves, for the sake of our children. And having learned what *gratitude* is meant that our children were on their way to becoming generous and gracious givers *themselves*.

We first learn to say "thank you" as a sort of rule or law imposed from the outside. Parents ask, "What do you say, Tommy?" when Aunt Clara gives a birthday gift. And the prompting results in what is at first, I suppose, a sort of obligatory acknowledgment of the gift. The words "thank you" fulfill the social requirements, earn the approval of other people. But we can usually tell when it is nothing more than a perfunctory response, as when one of our children who shall remain nameless this past week proposed to write a thank-you letter to his uncle telling him that he was pleased that his uncle had finally granted an over-due increase in his customary birthday gift of a *five*-dollar bill up to a *ten*-dollar bill. The mother of this child of ours who shall remain nameless let him know in rather forceful terms that such a message was *not* an acceptable expression of gratitude. *True* gratitude is not something that is for sale to the highest bidder. *True* gratitude springs from receiving *every* good thing that comes our way as a *gift*, not as something that is *due* or *deserved* or *earned*. True gratitude is not a matter of social obligation. It is a habit of the heart.

The Old Testament prophets looked at the events of their times and saw in them the hand of God. When, for instance, Judah fell to the Babylonians and Jerusalem was destroyed and many of the people were carried off into exile, the prophets detected in the catastrophe God's judgment upon the sins of their nation after long generations of warnings about their misconduct. There were plenty of people around who assured each other that they themselves had not done anything wrong—who denied that what had happened to them had any connection at all with behavior and attitudes—"What have *we* done? We don't *deserve* this!" And of those who *did* admit a connection between their way of life and the conquest of their nation—between their society's mistreatment of the poor and the profaning of worship and the punishment that had been inflicted—they all denied any *personal* role in the nation's sins. "*I* had nothing to do with it. It was my *neighbor's* fault. And I *certainly* had nothing to do with the sins of my parents' generation and their parents' generation before them, if *that's* what this is all about."

In fact, it seems, there was a common saying about the calamities that had befallen the people that interpreted the exile as a punishment for the sins of previous generations. It had become proverbial:

> The *parents* have eaten sour grapes,
> and the *children's* teeth are set on edge. (Jer 31:29)

The *parents* committed the *offense*, but the *children* are made to bear the *consequences*. The ancient Hebrews believed that sin was not just a *personal* matter, but a *social* one, so that doing *right* was a *collective* responsibility and doing *wrong* was a *collective* failure, one that even crossed generations, at least in God's eyes. After all, hadn't God said, "I will punish your sins unto the umpty-umpth generation?" But even if God *hadn't* said it, they could have observed, as is true today, that the weight of a society's sins are often felt by generations long after the fact. That's the nature of wrongdoing. It's a natural outcome. There is no such thing as a private sin; sin always taints relationships, it always has social implications, which frequently affect succeeding generations. Take for instance in the case of our own society's history, slavery, not only as an institution but as thousands upon thousands of individual instances, the effects of which we still cannot quite get out from under. Could it be that we are still feeling God's judgment for the behavior of generations long dead, nearly a century and a half after the Emancipation Proclamation?

That must have been a pretty dismal prospect for the ancient Jews, not only to be told that the defeat of their armies and the ruin of their farms and the devastation of their cities and the exile of their people to a far-away land were God's punishment upon *sin*, but that the punishment could be expected to *continue*, for sins that had taken place long ago in the past—breaking the laws that God had caused to be carved on stone and caused to be inscribed on scrolls. They must have felt pretty hopeless. The covenant that God had made with Abraham and renewed with Abraham's son Isaac and Isaac's son Jacob about having a land of their own, the covenant that God made with David the king and renewed with David's successors that theirs would be an everlasting throne in Israel, seemed to have been terminated because of what their ancestors had done, and the current generation could do nothing about it, was being made to suffer and even die for the sins of their parents and their parents' parents. So, their land was invaded and their farms were ruined and their buildings were burned down and their people were scattered and their society dismantled because generations had abused the Lord's favor. They had oppressed the poor and the outcast. They had worshiped wealth and prejudices. They had not done justice and worshiped rightly the God who had brought them prosperity and called them to mercy. All appeared hopeless. God's love seemed exhausted.

But then the prophets began to declare a *new* message to the people whose ancestors they had long warned of the judgment that was to come and finally *did* come with the fall of Jerusalem. On the *other* side of judgment, on the far side of despair and devastation, the prophets promised, was God's redemption. All that had befallen them by God's decree was actually for the purpose of preparing the way for God's salvation. What God had pulled down, God would restore.

> The days are surely coming, says the Lord, when I will sow the house of Israel and the house of Judah with the seed of humans and the seed of animals. And just as I have watched over them to pluck up and break down, to overthrow, destroy, and bring evil, so I will watch over them to build and to plant, says the Lord. In those days they shall no longer say:

> "The parents have eaten sour grapes,
> and the children's teeth are set on edge."
> But all shall die for *their own* sins; the teeth of everyone who eats sour grapes shall be set on edge. (31:27–30)

In other words, there will be no more condemnation because of what *others* have done.

Even *that* would be an improvement from the way things had worked out. But better than that,

> The days are surely coming, says the LORD, when I will make a *new* covenant with the house of Israel and the house of Judah. It will not be like the covenant that I made with their ancestors when I took them by the hand to bring them out of the land of Egypt—a covenant that they broke, though I was their husband, says the LORD. But this is the covenant that I will make with the house of Israel after those days, says the LORD: I will put my law within them, and I will write it on their hearts; and I will be their God, and they shall be my people. No longer shall they teach one another, or say to each other, "Know the LORD," for they shall *all* know me, from the least of them to the greatest, says the LORD; for I will forgive their iniquity, and remember their sin no more. (31:31–34)

No more will their obedience to my will be a matter of obeying a law chiseled on cold stone, God was saying. Their motive for obeying me will be love. Or, to put it another way, no longer will they say "Thank you, Daddy" out of a grudging sense of obligation, but out of a habit of gratitude in their hearts. On the other side of judgment, God's people will know God's intention for creation, and will celebrate it with every word and deed.

Christians recognize Jesus Christ as being the *embodiment* of God's new covenant that Jeremiah foretold. God's way with people on the other side of judgment would not only be a restoration of the promise of a land and a nation. God's way with people would be an indwelling love of God's truth, a habit of justice and peace, a thirst for righteousness not imposed by ordinance or by statute, but arising from a heart overflowing with gratitude for God's gracious and merciful ways with God's people. It would mean that God is no longer distant, but as close as our next breath. It would mean forgiveness and reconciliation. It would mean hope and joy. It would be a new beginning that would have no end, but an eternal fellowship with God that even death could not destroy. And the power of the Holy Spirit would write the terms of this *new* covenant on every receptive heart. God never punishes without redeeming. God stands on the other side of judgment, faithful to his purpose, just as God stands on *this* side of judgment, faithful to his purpose. And so, whatever befalls us as the consequence of sin, God is ready and able to work salvation. Only when the exiled people of Judah began to *understand* that promise did they find the hope and the courage to return from exile to the promised land and seek to rebuild their society in accordance with the blueprints of justice and peace, and to hope confidently for the Messiah who would lead them into the kingdom of God.

We could easily expect divine displeasure to lead first to divine rage and then to divine revenge. After all, that's how *we* instinctively tend to respond. On the other side of *human judgment, human nature* seeks *destruction*. Sometimes, all of us together enshrine that approach in our laws that mount penalty upon penalty, and we even pass laws that impose the *ultimate* penalty. But *God's* way—and the way to which God *calls* us—is that the other side of *judgment* is *redemption*. The Bible declares that God's response is restoration, rehabilitation, a new *beginning* after judgment has been pronounced. After *we* try to *reject God*, God binds himself even more tightly to us, even, ultimately, sending his own Son to die for our salvation, to clear away the obstacle of death, the last impediment to eternal life with God. The *old* covenant was in shambles. God's purpose seemed defeated—the people whom God had raised up and established had turned away in ungrateful disobedience and thankless rejection of everything that God desires. What would happen next? Would God understandably wash his hands of humankind and be done with it? Or would God be faithful to God's loving purpose? Was God's *judgment* the *last* word, the prelude to *destruction*, or was there *another* side of God's judgment, so that it is the prelude to *salvation*?

> The days are surely coming, says the Lord, when I will make a new covenant with the house of Israel and the house of Judah. It will not be like the covenant that I made with their ancestors when I took them by the hand to bring them out of the land of Egypt—a covenant that they broke, though I was their husband, says the Lord. But this is the covenant that I will make with the house of Israel after those days, says the Lord: I will put my law within them, and I will write it on their hearts; and I will be their God and they shall be my people. No longer shall they teach one another, or say to each other, "Know the Lord," for they shall *all* know me, from the *least* of them to the greatest, says the Lord; for I will forgive their iniquity, and remember their sin no more. (31:31–34)

The new covenant has been established in the life, death, and resurrection of Christ, and in the coming of the Holy Spirit into the hearts of every believer to inspire faith and to empower obedience, and now the kingdom of God is experienced in every habitual deed of love that springs from gratitude for what God has done for us. It is not a guarantee that we will never sin again, but a pledge that we *will* be forgiven. You and I and all people are invited to live in the peace and joy and hope that are God's promise on the other side of judgment. Now every deed we do, every thought we think, every word we utter, can be a way of saying, "Thank you, Father."

Thirtieth Sunday in Ordinary Time
First Presbyterian Church, Dodge City, Kansas
October 29, 1995

Joel 2:23–32
2 Timothy 4:6–8, 16–18
Luke 18:9–14

"Measuring Up to Heaven"

If you listen carefully to the words of Second Timothy, you can almost hear the heavy clang of chains and the booming thud of stout doors swinging shut and the gruff voices of the guards barking orders and the terrified moans of prisoners being dragged from their cells to meet some dreaded fate and the constant dripping of water seeping through the roof. You can imagine the smells of the place—dank air unsweetened by sunlight, made heavier with the odors of unwashed clothes and unwashed men and human waste. You can practically feel the cold stone walls and the cold bare floor and the cold iron bars. You can visualize the monotonous sameness of a dim chamber and the shadowy scurryings of roaches and beetles and spiders and rats. And a man sitting in the gloom with a pen or a stylus in hand, writing to his friend and colleague, begging him to come to the place, and to bring other friends and colleagues with him, perhaps for a final moment of comradeship and a last set of instructions before . . . .

He might have been an honored member of his community, this man, comfortably fixed in life, consulted on a variety of topics by his fellow citizens out of deference to his education and his insight. He had, in fact, been trained as a Pharisee back in Palestine, and his studies were no small accomplishment. He was proud of his Jewish heritage, and he was proud to be a Roman citizen, both. He had been respected, he had been sought out, a scholar who was zealous to uphold the community traditions and the pillars of faith. Who would know it to see him now, sitting in a Roman jail cell, a *criminal* in the eyes of the law, a *traitor* in the eyes of his countrymen, a *heretic* in the eyes of his religion, perhaps fighting not to be considered a failure in his own eyes and in the eyes of his friends, hopeful that he would *not* be considered a failure in the eyes of his Lord? He sensed that the end of his life was near—his life in this *earthly* existence, at any rate—and he was wondering to himself how he had measured up. Had he disappointed his family? Had he executed his responsibilities in life, and had he fulfilled his opportunities? Very likely, the *world's* answer would be *different* from that of the *believers* he had evangelized. Which opinion really mattered? Surely, in the end, only *God's* verdict on his life was the one to be concerned about. And yet . . . .

No, it was pointless to think of the "And yet's." That was the faithless part of him talking. He had followed his convictions. That was the best that a person could do. And especially if his convictions were grounded in the revelation of the one true God, and *God's* judgment of what is important in life. There could be no "And yet" comparable to his certainty in the lordship of Jesus Christ. If some would fault him for the decisions that he made as a missionary, then so be it; he could probably think of a hundred things that he wished he had done differently, but his conviction that Christ had called him to his work and that the Holy Spirit had sustained him in it was, in the end, unshakable. And whatever errors he had made, he trusted to the mercy of a God who had already forgiven him for no less a crime than persecuting the church established by God's own Son. He would pass on whatever wisdom he had gained in years of following the risen Christ and trusting in the ever-living God. Steadiness in the work, he wrote to his protégé, and endurance of suffering—these were key to the work of the evangelist in a hostile place and time. That is how the younger man would *fulfill his* ministry. It was not a theoretical ideal, but a page from the veteran missionary's own life experience. "As for me, I am already being poured out as a libation," Paul wrote to Timothy; "and the time of my departure has come. I have fought the good fight, I have finished the race, I have kept the faith" (2 Tim 4:6–7).

What more could anyone hope to say about a successful life? Compared with that, fame and fortune were irrelevant. What were a lavish table and a trunk full of jewels to a person who had run life's gauntlet and managed to keep the faith? "From now on there is reserved for me the crown of righteousness, which the Lord, the righteous judge, will give me on that day, and not only to me but also to all who have longed for his appearing" (4:8). Not that any of his accomplishments were his own doing—not even his faithfulness. "The Lord stood by me and gave me strength, so that through me the message might be fully proclaimed," he attested, "and all the Gentiles might hear it" (4:17a–b). And no blessing yet to come would be other than the Lord's doing. "The Lord will rescue me from every evil attack and save me for his heavenly kingdom. To him be the glory for ever and ever. Amen" (4:18). Nothing that he could have done on his own would have entitled him to enter heaven; his strength to preach the gospel in spite of threat and ridicule was from the Lord, and his strength to endure the sounds and smells and sights of his prison cell and whatever judgment the court would render came from the Lord, too. Paul's role had been to run the race set before him, trusting that the Lord had not called him to his faith and his work in vain. And that is what Paul did—he ran the race set before him, trusting in the Lord. If he measured up to heaven, the yardstick was not his own achievements, but the gracious faithfulness of Jesus Christ his Lord.

That was a long way for a Pharisee to come, trusting not in his *own* goodness, but in the goodness of God through Jesus Christ. Paul would have been habituated to thinking of his own *law-keeping* as his qualification for heaven, until the incident on the Damascus road. From that day forward, the Holy Spirit had tutored him in the lessons of grace. He was not a bad man before he encountered the risen Christ, but he was doing the wrong things out of the best of motives. Worst of all, even worse than persecuting the church, Paul would have been accustomed to measuring the distance he had to travel to heaven in comparison with the distance he supposed *others* had to travel, and he would have found *himself* always on heaven's doorstep, and the *lawbreakers* always far behind in the dust. But as Paul approached the end of life, when the ship of his soul would finally be cut free from its earthly moorings, he could look back on his years of trying to serve Christ faithfully and see that it was not his *own* feet that had carried him successfully to the finish line—nothing that *he* had done or said—but only the grace of God in Jesus Christ who had always been faithful to him, loving him, encouraging him, forgiving him. And the same love and encouragement and forgiveness that Paul might have been tempted from time to time to take for granted or to ignore entirely are precious and effective for *anyone* and *everyone* who has faith in Jesus Christ.

The Pharisees were inclined to trust in their *own* goodness and look down upon those whom they considered to be sinners, unworthy of heaven. It was in the company of Pharisees, or people *like* the Pharisees, that Jesus told a parable about two men, a Pharisee and a tax collector. They had both gone into the temple to pray. The Pharisee, who probably prayed there quite regularly, gave thanks to God, sincerely, for being so good to him. He did *not* confess his *sin*; according to *his* way of thinking, he *had* no sins to confess. He kept the commandments, and all the other details of the law, as well. He even fasted twice weekly, he even gave a tithe of all his income—gross, before taxes. He wouldn't think of associating with extortioners or the unjust or adulterers or tax collectors, like the tax collector who had entered the temple when he did and was praying far off in a corner, away from the altar, his eyes downcast. And well he *should* be praying, confessing his many sins. It must have irked the Pharisee, though, to think that *his* dutiful expression of piety by the altar necessarily brought him into the company of sinners like the tax collector. He would have appreciated having *two* temples in town—one for respectable people like himself, and one for the people who had *plenty* to confess.

Probably, the tax collector would not even have *noticed* the Pharisee. His thoughts were too wrapped up in himself and his need for God's mercy. He knew that he was far from perfect in God's eyes, a long way from heaven's doorstep. And so, *he* had something *really* to pray about, one simple but fervent sentence in Jesus' parable: "'God, be merciful to me, a sinner!'" (Luke 18:13b). In *his* self-satisfied *complacency*, the *Pharisee* had told God in prayer how little *he needed* God. In *his* self-despising urgency, the tax collector had told God how little *he deserved* heaven. "I tell you," said Jesus, "this man went down to his home justified rather than the other" (18:14a). The way we measure up to heaven, it seems, is by acknowledging how far we are away from it and despairing of our *own* ability to run that distance. Only *then* can we be *truly* thankful for God's mercy in Jesus Christ.

Since *his* days as a Pharisee, Paul had had many humbling experiences—being jeered at, being stoned, being arrested, being jailed, now being jailed again. We marvel that such abuse did not turn him *away* from the Christ who had called him into such a life. We are amazed that he showed no signs of longing for the old days of comfort and esteem. We are astounded that his experiences only made him more *grateful* for the love and mercy of God in Jesus Christ and for the gifts of endurance and fortitude with which God had endowed him through the Holy Spirit. We think of *our* trials—the *serious* ones, not the *trivial* ones—and we consider how *we* are tempted just to give *up* on Christian hope and give *in* to the self-centeredness and greed and meanness of the world, perhaps supposing that, burdened as we are, *our* way in life should be easier. We think of the sins that we read about in newspapers and see on television and are aware of in the house next door, and we consider how *we* would *never* think of committing murder or theft or adultery—conveniently overlooking our gossip and our envy and our lust—perhaps supposing that, good as we are, *our* way to heaven should be shorter, certainly *must* be shorter than for all those *real* sinners. Careful, Jesus warns us and Paul discovered: it is not *our goodness* that makes us fit for salvation, but *God's mercy*. Beware lest we consider ourselves over-qualified for heaven, and so run right by heaven's door in a race that we think we are winning on our *own* strength.

If you listen carefully to the words of Second Timothy, you can hear, *over* the heavy clang of chains and the booming thud of stout doors swinging shut and the gruff voices of the guards barking orders and the terrified moans of prisoners being dragged from their cells to meet some dreaded fate and the constant dripping of water seeping through the roof, a lone prisoner singing brightly and contentedly of his trust in God's goodness, ending in the Gloria Patri. "The Lord stood by me and gave me strength" (2 Tim 4:17a), goes his song. "The Lord will rescue me from every evil attack and save me for his heavenly kingdom. To him be the glory for ever and ever. Amen" (4:18). You can imagine that in that cell, his sweetness of spirit has sponged all dankness from the atmosphere as he has raised prayers for the forgiveness of whoever has wronged him in any way. You can practically feel the glowing heart of faith warming even the stones and the floor and the bars. You can visualize a person whose gaze is piercing the gloom of a jail cell and fixing upon the heavenly crown of righteousness within his grasp. And you can understand that *our* measuring up to heaven has very *little* to do with earning points for our own law-keeping and our own goodness, and has *everything* to do with God's merciful love and the goodness of Jesus Christ.

All Saints' Day

First Presbyterian Church, Ponca City, Oklahoma
November 1, 2013

Daniel 7:1–3, 15–18
Ephesians 1:11–23
Luke 6:20–31

"No Church, No Body"

There are many joys in professional ministry. To be called to be an apostle, a prophet, a shepherd, a servant of Christ, is an amazing privilege to begin with, and then to experience being an instrument in God's miraculous awakening of people to faith and understanding, to be welcomed into the profound and intimate moments of people's birth and death and the commitments and celebrations and sorrows in between, to experience on a regular basis being lifted out of oneself and pulled beyond one's narrow wants and desires and abilities—all of these are reasons for deep and abiding joy.

But there are also some *sadnesses* in the ministry—wounds and bruises when one feels mistreated, surely, but also some real heartaches over the situation of others. I think my greatest sadness is when I hear from someone that he or she sees no reason to be a part of Christ's church. I cannot count the number of times I have met with a family following a death and am told that their loved one believed in God, for sure, but, no, they didn't have much to do with the church, didn't worship with others, cherished the Bible but never much got around to reading it, devoted their attention to their work and their own family and therefore didn't really have time much to spend on people outside their own household.

There's the *practical* issue—how does one prepare a Christian funeral around a life of inattention to the matters of Christian faith? There's the *personal* issue—wasn't it a waste to have missed out on the joy of a vocation beyond simply punching a timeclock and cashing a paycheck, forgoing the warmth of family ties that stretch around the world and backward to the beginning of time and forward through all eternity? Then there's also the *theological* issue—how can one claim to love Christ while denying him his continuing presence in the world which the church *is*? The choice *not* to be part of Christ's church is a choice to *reject* Christ's lordship and to *deprive* Christ of the fulfillment of his mission—in Matthew's Gospel, Jesus commended Peter as the rock upon which he would build his church—the church for whose life Christ died, as we testify in the great hymn "The Church's One Foundation." And the other Gospels and the book of Acts and all the letters of Paul and the other epistles in the New Testament give witness to the fact that the church is not just a name given to scattered believers who do not worship together and who do not have fellowship with one another and who do not study together and who do not pray together and who do not plan and conduct mission together.

To be baptized is to be made one with Christ in his life and in his death, *and* to be engrafted into his church. And on this day each year, November 1, the church celebrates and gives thanks for all of those who have responded to the call and have been receptive to the Holy Spirit to live out the truth of their baptism faithfully, some of whom incurred poverty and disease in the course of their discipleship, and even withering death, some of whom met persecution in the course of their faithfulness, and even violent death, and are considered martyrs. But the channel through which they served faithfully—the source of the prayers that supported them and the nurturing home that formed them—was Christ's church, and the worship through which they voiced thanksgiving and praise to God and the setting in which they confessed their sins to God and asked for God's pardon and the table at which they found reconciliation and were nourished for faithful service was the church's.

The letter to the Ephesians is sometimes referred to as the epistle of the Holy Spirit, and sometimes as the epistle of the church. Indeed, it could not be one without also being the other. *Every* book and letter in the New Testament gives witness to the power of the Holy Spirit. *Every* book and letter in the New Testament assigns great importance to the church. But *Ephesians*, as no other part of the New Testament, emphatically declares the significance of the church as the means through which the Holy Spirit works God's heavenly will and Christ's continuing ministry in the world that God is in the ongoing process of redeeming. "I pray that the God of our Lord Jesus Christ, the Father of glory, may give you a spirit of wisdom and revelation as you come to know him," we read in Ephesians, so that, with the eyes of your heart enlightened, you may know what is the hope to which he has called you, what are the riches of his glorious inheritance among the saints, and what is the immeasurable greatness of his power for us who believe, according to the working of his great power. God put this power to work in Christ when he raised him from the dead and seated him at his right hand in the heavenly places, far above all rule and authority and power and dominion, and above every name that is named, not only in this age but also in the age to come. And he has put all things under his feet and has made him the *head* over all things *for the church, which is his body,* the *fullness* of him who fills all in all. (Eph 1:17–23)

The church does not exalt itself, must not exalt itself, has no *reason* to exalt itself. It exalts *Christ* and proclaims what Christ has achieved and is achieving. But what Christ has achieved and is achieving, Christ has done through the church, is doing through the church. It is his body, we read time and again in scripture. Christ is the *head* of the body, but the church is Christ's hands and feet, eyes and ears. It is the task of the *church* to be alert and active in the world that Jesus no longer inhabits in his physical earthly form. Christ ascended into heaven, to sit at the right hand of God the Father. The Bible declares it. We confess it in our creeds. He still *has* a body on earth, but that body is the *church*, of which Christ is the *head*. How can anyone deny its importance—indeed, its necessity? If there were no church, of what would Christ be the head? If there were no church, there would be no body. If there were no body, Christ would be no more than a name on the page of a history book, his teachings merely nice thoughts, his healings a fairy tale, his forgiveness a wish. The incarnation—the enfleshment of the will and purpose of God in Jesus of Nazareth—continues today, two thousand years after the ascension, in the church.

That is not to say that the church has always been faithful, or that it has always been obedient. The church has been a perpetrator of some of the most wickedly un-Christ-like events in history and has been shamefully silent in the face of many others. Even today, it profits financially through investments and otherwise from activities that scandalize the faith and mock its creeds. It is far from perfect. When, at times, it has bullied, when, at times, it has been distracted from ministering to the genuine needs of people, when, at times, it has departed from the truth that there is but one Messiah of God, one Lord, one Savior, when, at times, it has shielded tyrants or neglected the poor, then it has *suffered* from the compromise of its witness, and so has the *world*. But it is the church faithful, the body of Christ, that educated women and minorities when many thought it unnecessary. It is the church faithful, the body of Christ, that built hospitals for lepers and sat with the victims of AIDS and sent out medical missionaries who put their lives in jeopardy for the sake of healing some. It is the church faithful, the body of Christ, that stood up for the working poor when slumlords and inhumane industrialists treated men, women, and children as less than the image of God. And it is the church faithful *still*, the body of Christ *still*, that shows compassionate mercy, that binds up the wounded, that feeds the hungry, that comforts the afflicted, and confronts any and all who would obstruct the fullness of the kingdom of God, all in the name of, and in obedience to, Jesus Christ. And it is the church faithful *still*, the body of Christ *still*, that willingly gives up its *own* privileges in the service of the one who gave up *his* life for the salvation of the world.

Over the past few months, people of all faiths and no faith have been intrigued with a new pope who has renewed the call of Roman Catholics and any other Christians who will listen to the ministry of compassionate mercy, binding up the wounded, feeding the hungry, comforting the afflicted, confronting any and all who would obstruct the fullness of the kingdom of God, thereby glorifying the name of Jesus Christ and demonstrating obedience to him. Just a few weeks ago, Pope Francis called upon his branch of the church to give up its own privileges in the service of the one who gave up his *life* for the salvation of the world. Jesus declared God's promise to the poor, to the hungry, to the sorrowful, to the reviled and the slandered. There are some things, and inevitably will continue to be some things, over which Presbyterians and other Protestants will have fundamental differences with the Roman Catholic Church and its supreme bishop. But as the world hears and sees an emphasis on the priorities of Christ, as scripture bears witness, being therefore also the priorities of Christ's *church*, it will learn that the church is indeed the body of Christ still present and ministering faithfully in the world that God *created*, that God *loves*, *on* which God showers *blessings*, *for* which God has sacrificed that which was most *dear*, *to* which God has promised a destiny of *transformation* and *renewal*. To all of that, perhaps surprisingly, certainly miraculously, and absolutely graciously, the church is central, for it is the body of Christ.

All the saints of all the ages, not perfect but faithful, not praising themselves but pointing always and only to Jesus Christ, are present with us here tonight—can you sense it?—gathered at this table, the image of the heavenly banquet table around which they now feast eternally in joyful company with their risen and living Lord. They have graduated from their earthly role as Jesus' eyes and ears, hands and feet, but having given of themselves in service as Christ gave himself in service, so the church testifies that *we* are part of that great company of the faithful that sings praise eternally to the

Christ of God, our head. We are a part of that same church, the same body of Christ, through whom God's will and purpose are being worked out, by the power of the Holy Spirit, even right here in Ponca City, inheritors of the riches of grace, destined for salvation. As promised in the Revelation to John: "Blessed are the dead who die in the Lord, says the Spirit. They rest from their labors, and their deeds follow them."[1]

---

1. Rev 14:13 as in Office of Worship, *Funeral*, 26.

Thirty-first Sunday in Ordinary Time
Spanish Springs Presbyterian Church, Sparks, Nevada
November 4, 2007

Habakkuk 1:1–4; 2:1–4
2 Thessalonians 1:1–4, 11–12
Luke 19:1–10

"Touched by God"

On his way to Jerusalem, where he would die on a cross, the Son of God passed through the town of Jericho. He had just recently told his disciples once again about what would happen to him in the capital. But once again, the Bible tells us, the disciples did not understand. As they neared the town of Jericho, a blind man sitting alongside the road and begging for coins from passersby heard the crowd coming toward him. He asked what was going on, and someone told him that Jesus of Nazareth was approaching. The man shouted out to Jesus, but the people around him ordered him to be quiet. Undaunted, he shouted again, even more loudly, and Jesus heard him and asked that the man be brought to him, then inquired what it was that the man wanted of him. The man asked Jesus to restore his sight, and Jesus did so, and the man then joined the entourage as it entered the town. All who had witnessed the miracle, Luke tells us, "praised God" (Luke 18:43).

The crowd was growing. These people had heard about Jesus, and it's likely that this miracle right at the city limits attracted even *more* people to the parade. Another man was sitting at his desk in his office doing his usual work—an *unpopular* man, because his *job* was unpopular. He was a tax collector, and in ancient Palestine, tax collectors were in the service of Rome, the hated occupying power. Not only that, but tax collectors were free to charge exorbitant commissions for their service to Rome—commissions paid not by the *Romans* but by the taxpayers of *Palestine*. Because of their complicity with the pagan occupiers, and because of the very nature of their business, tax collectors, though Jews and fellow Israelites, were classed with robbers and murderers and adulterers and brothel-keepers. The man's name was Zacchaeus, which, ironically, meant "pure" or "righteous." Nobody *thought* of him that way, probably not even *himself*—surely he knew how much other people despised him.

The hubbub outside was apparently enough to draw Zacchaeus's attention away from his business. He came out onto the street and saw the crowd. It must have been an extraordinary event for the town, and as Zacchaeus was trying to discover what all the commotion was about, perhaps he heard snatches of the news about Jesus, perhaps even testimony about having seen the blind man's sight being restored just moments before.

Out of curiosity, or for a diversion, or perhaps because of some yearning for God, Zacchaeus decided that he would see this man for *himself* that people were so excited about. But the crowd was so large that he *couldn't* see the man at the center of it. The Sunday school song and the traditional translation of the story say it was because Zacchaeus was short of stature. The normal rules of Greek syntax, however, imply that it was actually *Jesus* who was short. In either case, the size of the crowd made it impossible for Zacchaeus, standing on the sidewalk, to see the person who was the center of attention. On an impulse, he decided to climb up a sycamore tree in order to see over the heads of the crowd. Surely, climbing trees was something that the chief tax collector of Jericho did not do very often—probably hadn't done since he was a boy—and this unconscious compromise of his dignity and hard-nosed businessman image was doubtless out of character and totally unexpected by the citizens of Jericho. There is no suggestion in the text that Zacchaeus was particularly trying to get Jesus' attention, but the antics of the man, well-dressed and clinging to a tree trunk or limb, could hardly have escaped Jesus' notice, and the notice of other people, too. "Look at Zacchaeus!" someone must have shouted. "I always *thought* Zacchaeus looked rather like a monkey," someone else might have commented. "Squeezing even the *figs* dry, are you, Zacchaeus?" another might have derided him. "I hope you fall and break your neck, Zacchaeus," an anonymous and more hostile voice might have called.

But the crowd's festive mood must have changed abruptly when Jesus came to the place and looked up and said to the man in the tree, "'Zacchaeus'"—surely Jesus would have heard the man's name by that time—"'hurry and come down; for I must stay at your house today'" (19:5b). Zacchaeus immediately complied, and "all who saw it began to grumble and said, 'He has gone to be the guest of one who is a *sinner*'" (19:7). Zacchaeus, though, did not notice their reproof of Jesus. His breathing was rapid. His heart was racing. He made haste to welcome Jesus and offer him hospitality—when was the last time that anyone in Jericho had wanted to enter Zacchaeus's home? Indeed, any righteous person would have considered it to be a place contaminated by Zacchaeus's sins, so that anybody *entering* it would be made unclean, too. I imagine that the crowd began to thin at this point. How had they been so duped as to waste their time on someone who could so freely have social intercourse with a tax collector? The miracles were immediately forgotten as some drifted away muttering to themselves, "Forget it!"

Zacchaeus would have known that he was not only *disliked* by others; he was considered a *sinner* by others. Had he tried to visit the synagogue, he would have been barred from entering, shunned by any self-respecting Jew out of concern that the man named "*Pure*" would so *sully* the place that it could never be cleansed of his immoral stench. But here was this visitor from out of town, doing things that only *prophets* were thought to be able to do—representatives of *God*—who had singled Zacchaeus out for the honor of hosting him during his stay. It was very likely the first *positive* attention that Zacchaeus had received from a fellow Jew during his entire adult life. And it is instructive that, at this sign of acceptance by Jesus, the very first words out of Zacchaeus's mouth were, "'Look, half of my possessions, Lord, I will give to the poor; and if I have defrauded anyone of anything, I will pay back four times as much'" (19:8).

We in modern America seem to think that everything has a price tag on it. Even human life has come to be assessed in terms of dollars—when someone, by negligence or intentionally, causes the death of another, that person can be sued for damages, often in the millions of dollars. Our first cynical reaction to Zacchaeus's offer—perhaps as the townspeople's first cynical reaction to Zacchaeus's offer would have been—might be to say, "So he thinks he can make up for all his sins by paying money!" But Jesus hadn't judged Zacchaeus, certainly had not condemned him. Just the opposite—he had singled him out for what you and I would agree was a very great honor. Zacchaeus wasn't paying a *fine* because he had been found *guilty*. He was *offering* his goods and money because he felt *blessed*—blessed to receive the kind and merciful attention of Jesus the healer, the teacher, the defender, the Son of God. "Jesus said to him, 'Today salvation has come to this house, because he too is a son of Abraham. For the Son of Man came to seek out and save the lost'" (19:9–10). Jesus didn't write out a receipt, "Payment received in cancellation of a *debt*." He acknowledged Zacchaeus's offer as an expression of his *faith*. Zacchaeus had responded to Jesus' acceptance of him in the manner in which he was most familiar—materially and monetarily—and in the terms of repentance for any sins he might have committed in the course of his business. Jesus had said nothing about sin—in fact, had treated Zacchaeus in just the opposite way from what anybody else who judged Zacchaeus to be a *sinner* would have done. It would have been obvious to Jesus what the townspeople thought of Zacchaeus, and he would certainly have known how tax collectors were popularly regarded. But Jesus saw in him a person who was included in the covenant God had made with Abraham many centuries before, and *his* concern was to dispense *salvation*, not *punishment*. Zacchaeus had confirmed Jesus' assessment; realizing that in Jesus' coming to him he had in fact been touched by God, Zacchaeus responded with generosity.

How is it with you? Have you come out of your house or place of business today, out of your daily routine and mundane cares, to see what the hubbub is about—that is, to try to get a glimpse of this man whom people have been talking about? And when you have done what you needed to do to try to get a good view of him—singing a hymn, saying a prayer, listening to a sermon—have you discovered (or at least suspected) that he was looking straight at you, straight into your eyes, straight into your mind and your heart, and saying, "Hurry and come down, for I must stay at *your* house today" (19:5b)? By doing so, he isn't speaking in condemnation, not threatening judgment, certainly not joining in any chorus of disapproval, but identifying you as a child of the covenant, as you were baptized to be, blessing you with his full attention and unconditional acceptance. And what will you do, once you have scrambled down out of your sycamore tree—your seat in the sanctuary—and found yourself face to face with the Son of God, touched by God's own blessing of love, the gift of himself? That's what this Dedication Sunday is really about. What will you do, who know yourself to have been touched by God in Jesus Christ?

Of all the people on the streets of Jericho that day, only Zacchaeus, ironically, came to know and understand what Jesus was all about. The others in the crowd were happy enough to follow Jesus as long as he was behaving in a way that agreed with their way of thinking, with their values and judgments. But, so far as we know, not one of them had offered anything in the way of a sacrifice, anything that would *cost* them, had not even offered him the hospitality of their home. Probably, not one of them thought him- or herself a sinner, at least not in any serious sense. And so, they did not take Jesus' presence among them, his conversation with them, at full value. Zacchaeus knew how much he *needed* someone like Jesus—and his mercy. And the instant he *received* it, he was overcome with joy and gratitude that flowed out in the natural channel of generosity. He wasn't bargaining for forgiveness—he had already received it, freely. He wasn't bidding for God's attention—he had already received that, too, freely. He was acting out of pure elation—the elation that anyone should feel when they know themselves to have been touched by God.

The Bible never mentions Zacchaeus again. It would be interesting to know what the people of Jericho came to think of him in the days after Jesus came to stay at his house. Did he follow through with his pledge to Jesus? I think so. Did he quit his job? I doubt it, but I think that, thereafter, he tried very hard to be fair and just. It might not have made a great difference in the way the *taxpayers* regarded him—they *still* would have grumbled about paying taxes, though they might not have been quite so disrespectful of him. But the point of the story isn't about *them*, about the self-satisfied people who *didn't* welcome the Son of God into their home. It's a story about Jesus and the response of people who know themselves to have been blessed, touched by God—about joy and gratitude and generosity. Jesus had deigned to stop at Zacchaeus's house and bless him with his gracious presence, and Zacchaeus responded to the honor. Jesus' *next* stop was Jerusalem—where he died on the cross for you.

Thirty-second Sunday in Ordinary Time

Haggai 1:15b—2:9
2 Thessalonians 2:1–5, 13–17
Luke 20:27–38

"The God of the Living"

"It's just what the tornado did *here*, only even worse," Wendy Palmer explained, recounting her recent trip to the Holy Land and her tour of the Temple Mount in Jerusalem. "All that's left of the temple, really, is the wall around the Temple Mount, and all these people come to pray there every day. The mosques up on top—they're beautiful, though the people who worship up there, Muslims, have to go through all this security and are always under strict surveillance and the government shuts off their access from time to time. But it wasn't Muslims, of course, who destroyed the Jewish temple. It was the Romans, thirty or forty years after the death of Jesus. But it reminded me so much of what happened to our church."

"Well, our church *building*, anyway," Reverend Miller responded. "The *church* is still here. *We're* still here, though the building was destroyed. And that was a great loss. But the church is first and foremost the people, and, thank goodness, none of us was killed or even hurt, or other people in town, either."

"That was certainly a miracle," Wendy Palmer observed.

"A lot have moved away, though," interjected Tony Simmons. "And they won't be coming back. Left for the big cities, most of them. They'll stay where they've got jobs. And they took their money with them."

"It'll never be like it was," Anna Wilson added, sighing. "The insurance people have made that pretty clear."

"It doesn't mean that it won't be very good," Reverend Miller observed. "It will be different, yes, not as ornate perhaps, but a suitable house for worshiping God and teaching about God and just enjoying being God's people together."

"But we can't replace the memories," Tony Simmons said.

"And so many things that our parents and aunts and uncles and grandparents contributed, all gone now," Anna Wilson sighed again, her eyes starting to glisten with tears.

"We ought to put every dollar into making the new sanctuary just exactly the way it was," John Collins asserted. "That's what's important. Not all this extra stuff, like that youth center business."

"But the youth center was a part of the old building, too," observed Wendy Palmer. "We need *all* those things, and the *town* needs them, too. My children loved coming to all the activities in the youth center, and the town will need a place for wholesome youth events even more now that just about every other youth gathering spot has been damaged or destroyed. The high school gym is gone, and the auditorium. What are the kids to do, especially if the ballpark and skating rink and arts pavilion don't get rebuilt? And if they do eventually get replaced, it's not going to be soon enough to be available to *today's* youth. They will have missed out on so much of what childhood and youth should be about."

The class had obviously gotten off track. It was supposed to be an opportunity for Wendy Palmer to report on her journey to Israel and Palestine, but, like so much about Centerville, the class agenda had become dominated by the storm that had devastated much of the town a few months earlier. The church building, long a fixture in the town, both architecturally and socially, as well as spiritually, had been devastated. The sanctuary, more than a hundred years old but well maintained and an architectural gem listed on the state's register of historic places, had been utterly destroyed, as had the church's fellowship hall and youth center, which had had a basketball court and game rooms and had been a gathering place for the community's youth every weekend, not just the children of the congregation. The Christian education wing was relatively unscathed, miraculously and thanks to the caprice of the tornadic winds, but had not yet been authorized for use by local safety officials and would require some basic cosmetic repairs. After assessment by the insurance adjuster, it was clear that the entire building had been significantly underinsured for many years—the budget always seemed to require across-the-board economizing—and it was also clear that materials and builders would be at a premium for some time, limiting repairs and reconstruction not only in Centerville, but in all of the surrounding damaged communities, as well.

A portable building had been brought to the church site to accommodate worship and a couple of classes before the service, but many regular worshipers stayed away, waiting, as they said, for a "real church" before they would return. The adult class was meeting in the Simmons' living room, but one of the customary participants was confined to a wheelchair and could not gain easy access up the front stairs and through the narrow doorway, and had elected not to try to attend.

"All the beautiful stained glass and the carved wood," Anna Wilson sighed again.

"That's what drew people," John Collins added. "We have to have a beautiful sanctuary, at least as magnificent as it was before."

"But the children!" Wendy Palmer appealed. "We can worship in a youth center, but you can't play basketball in a sanctuary."

Reverend Miller was frustrated by the debate that had been going on within the congregation now for several weeks, which had also paralyzed a session reluctant to offend any of the church members, all of whose financial support was vital to any rebuilding program, let alone maintaining the intangibles of congregational life. "Perhaps we could allow Wendy to continue with her report of her trip," he ventured. The debate ceased, but there remained a palpable mood of discontent in the room.

"You know," Wendy Palmer noted, "Judaism survived the destruction of the temple by the Romans, like it had survived the destruction of the temple of David by the Babylonians. Our tour guide talked a lot about that."

"I don't see what that has to do with our situation," John Collins said, unwilling to leave the topic of how to get on with rebuilding.

"We would be dishonoring our forebears," Anna Wilson said, "if we didn't devote every bit of our time and energy and money to rebuilding the sanctuary exactly like it was. It's like spitting on their graves."

"That's going a little far," objected Fred Morris, who up until now had kept his silence throughout the morning's discussion, as he did most Sundays. "I don't think we should hobble the future by speculating about the wishes of dead people."

"How can you say such a horrible thing?" Anna Wilson asked, obviously shocked to the core of her being.

"I mean no disrespect," Fred Morris said. "I've only been here about twelve years, and I admit I didn't know all these people you remember, people obviously important in the history of this church and of this town. But we're in danger of worshiping a structure, I think."

Reverend Miller decided it was time to intervene again. "What is it that our ancestors were building here, and why? I think that's important to think about. Yes, they sacrificed much for this church building and for this town. But what was their motive, do we think? What was their purpose? It might help, in considering all of this, to reflect on what the Bible says about rebuilding the temple in Jerusalem when the exiles returned from Babylon. Several of the books of the Old Testament address that."

"And a rebuilt temple that itself was destroyed almost two thousand years ago and has never been built again," observed Wendy Palmer.

"The sanctuary must be rebuilt," said John Collins. "It must come first. And anything else right now would delay that, maybe make it impossible."

"The session is looking at our options, taking all of our needs into consideration," said Reverend Miller.

John Collins grumbled something unintelligible, but no one asked him to repeat it.

"You know," Fred Morris spoke again, "at this very moment, over in the portable, we have a couple of dedicated church members who are teaching a children's class and a youth class, in the same room and without tables and other things that we all took for granted in Sunday school, not ideal conditions, but trying mightily to help the younger generation to know about Jesus, and not a one of those kids knew any of the people who built and maintained the sanctuary over the decades. I think an important question is what *their* memories of this church will be when they're *our* age, making decisions about making the effort to raise their own children in the church, this one or some other one. Will it depend upon stained glass and carved wood, or upon something else?"

Wendy Palmer spoke up. "Does anyone else remember Mr. Stanton, the youth choir director back in the 1970s?" Several heads nodded. "He's the one who convinced me that I could sing. And he always used to take time in our rehearsal to talk about *what* we were singing—what the hymns and anthems were saying, both the words and the notes, and why it was important, and about the importance of helping to lead the congregation in worship. I think much of what I know about Christianity, I learned from the music we sang with him. He was always so patient with us and made us realize what an important part of the church we were."

The class fell silent, until Sherry Quincy, often a reflective and reconciling voice, said, "I don't recall noticing much about the sanctuary when I was a child, but I remember Mrs. Downing, and how she came to visit us when my mother died." She paused to wipe a tear from one eye. "Did any of you have Mrs. Downing in church school, too?"

A few heads nodded, and smiles came to lips.

"She was one of the first people to come to the house. And she just hugged me and assured me that God would take care of my mom, and would take care of us, too, my dad and my brother and me. And then, over the years, she would make a point of telling me how proud my mother would have been of me, and how she saw the Holy Spirit at work in my life—not on any particular special occasion, either—just, you know . . . ."

The class fell quiet again for a few minutes. Then John Collins broke the silence. "I remember *Dr.* Downing. He came to the youth group one time, and we were divided up, the girls going off with somebody I don't remember, and Dr. Downing sat with the boys and talked about, well, I guess you would call it sex education today. Everybody was kind of nervous and embarrassed, but I guess it was something the youth leaders arranged for every few years. Anyway, I don't remember much of the specifics"—here, he broke off and chuckled self-consciously, and others in the room chuckled as well—"but I remember how he ended his talk. 'Always remember, when you're out on a date, to treat your date as a child of God, and as if Jesus was there with you. Because he is.'" John Collins shook his head meditatively. "And I remember Bill Morris—some of you might have known him before his family moved away" (at this, some heads nodded). "Anyway, I remember how Bill took me aside when we were on a double date once and things were getting, well, kind of romantic, you might say, and reminded me of what Dr. Downing had told us all about Christ being there with us. I guess that's one of the strongest memories about what this church means to me." He paused, then added, "Maybe even more than those magnificent windows. Even the one that my great-grandparents donated."

The room fell silent again. Eventually, Tony Simmons spoke. "The church is a place of memory, for sure, all the good things that went before. But I guess it really needs to dedicate its resources to what will make a positive difference for the living."

"We are assured that the faithful who have gone before us live forever with Jesus in the presence of God," Reverend Miller said after a few moments during which all were thinking about what they owed to their ancestors, and to those just starting out in life, and to those yet to come. "Thanks be to the God of the living."

John Collins clasped his hands and bowed his head.

Thirty-third Sunday in Ordinary Time

First Presbyterian Church, Dodge City, Kansas

November 19, 1995

Isaiah 65:17–25
2 Thessalonians 3:6–13
Luke 21:5–19

"This Is Good News?"

What television programs make you laugh? Some time ago, I discovered a British comedy on our local public television station called *Bless Me, Father*. It was a show about a veteran Roman Catholic priest and his curate who had just entered the priesthood and their life in a parish in southern England shortly after the Second World War. Perhaps being in the ministry made it especially pertinent for me, but, for whatever reason, it quickly became a favorite program; in fact, it was *one* of the reasons for buying a video tape recorder, to be able to capture the shows in order to be able to watch them over and over. I especially appreciated the fact that the program often touched on real theological issues and on the attitudes of mistrust and suspicion that characterized Catholic and Protestant relations in those days and are still a hurdle to ecumenical endeavors today.

One episode began with Father Duddleswell preaching to his assembled flock on the subject of the day of judgment. "Did you hear," he asked, "the good one about the fellow who died after a lifetime of thieving, drunkenness, and debauchery? One chappie at his funeral looked down at the coffin and said to his mate, 'Pat,' says he, 'the devil's got him at last.' 'Oh no, no, no, no, no, Tommy boy,' says Pat, 'you mustn't speak ill of the dead.' 'Not at all,' says Tommy. 'If the devil hasn't got that one down there, then there's no use in us keeping a devil at all.' Now I pray, my dear brethren," Father Duddleswell said as he concluded his sermon, "for you all to be chaste and holy, so you do not fall into the devil's black hands and be toasted worse than kippers and muffins. Imagine fire and brimstone for all eternity. And now we'll sing that beautiful hymn, number 159, 'Day of Wrath, O Day of Mourning.'"[1] The rest of the episode involved the young curate's attempt to repair the faith crisis that the crusty old priest's sermon produced among some parishioners who feared that their relatives died unforgiven of their sins.

Well, most of us don't begrudge God the right to do whatever God wants to do with notorious sinners. We may not talk so much in terms of fire and brimstone anymore, but our sense of justice allows most of us to accommodate the Bible's stark images of judgment. But we may have considerably more difficulty with the Bible's predictions of disaster which will befall the righteous innocent. We know that being a follower of Christ is no protection from heartache. In today's reading from Luke, Jesus seems to say that, as the end of history as we know it approaches, those who are *faithful* to him are virtually *guaranteed* of heartache—of arrest and persecution, betrayal and punishment, even death for some, and hatred for all.

Those who were with Jesus must have been astounded at such news. It had all started with an innocent comment about the temple. The simple folks who had followed Jesus up to the big city from the farms and docks and villages of *Galilee* were oohing and ahhing at this great wonder of the ancient world, as out-of-towners would. It was quite a spectacle—a huge monument to Israel's faith, but also to Herod's vanity, layered with gleaming marble and shining gold, filled with ornate furnishings and exquisite decoration. Jesus rather deflated his friends' pious awe when he told them, "Eh, it won't last. One day, like all human creations, it will be a heap of ruins." Imagine their shock that he could speak so irreverently about such a disaster ahead for the very hub of Israel's spiritual life! Immediately, they began to question him when this would be and what sign would precede it. Jesus refused to speculate about the timetable of destruction, but he *did* predict that there would be suffering and disaster before the end. And then, the real shocker—even *before* these terrible events of wars and earthquakes and famines and plagues, the followers of Jesus could expect trial and tribulation just because of their faithfulness. But when the disasters occurred, they must not lose their faith and they must not allow themselves to refrain from giving testimony to their faith. "You will be hated by all because of my name," Jesus told them, and then, curiously, "But not a hair of your head will perish. By your endurance you will gain your souls" (Luke 21:17–19).

---

1. Askey, "Fire and Brimstone."

By the time that Luke wrote his Gospel, Herod's Temple was already in a heap. Jerusalem had been surrounded by soldiers. The trampling of the city by the Gentile armies of Rome had caused the people to flee in dismay. By then, many a faithful Christian had been martyred, and many others had suffered alienation from family and friends, as Jesus had predicted, along with loss of reputation and perhaps loss of fortune. The evangelists had spoken of the message of Jesus as being Good News, but it must not have seemed like very good news to the faithful who were enduring in their daily lives fire and brimstone as frightening as any *hell* they could imagine. They needed to be reminded that this was all to be expected—the result not of their *sin*, but of their very *faithfulness* to Jesus Christ. They needed to remember that all of this was not God's promise gone *sour*, but the *sign* of God's trustworthiness. Jesus had *told* his followers that this is what it would be like. Jesus had *told* his followers that this was the prelude to the end time. They should not be fearful, they should not abandon their hope. All was as it must be. And that was reason to remain faithful through it all. What was important for the followers of Jesus to remember was that the terrors and great signs would not be the forerunners of God's total annihilation of creation, but evidence of the in-breaking of the promised messianic age. As a woman cannot give birth to a new being without great pain, so God's creation cannot take hold of the promise until its foundations are shaken. In both cases, the pain is a harbinger not of death, but of life. Why must it be this way? Scripture doesn't say. What it *does* say is that what appears to *us* as God's *curse* is, in reality, the necessary condition for God's *blessing*.

We know something of this truth from our personal experience—how God has laid hold of us and pulled us through the disappointment of a lost job or the heartbreak of a broken marriage to a new experience of blessing in a more satisfying occupation or a home of deep love and commitment. It is something like that, only on a grander cosmic scale, that *Jesus* was talking about. The disciple's concern is to make use of the time available not in profitless speculation, but in dedicated witnessing to the redemptive purpose of God. The whole creation stands at the window eagerly awaiting the arrival of the day of redemption for the children of God. Wars and earthquakes and famines and plagues are not to usher in a time of *terror* for the *faithful*, but to serve as signs of the time *and* of our salvation.

So, shall we pray for *more* wars and earthquakes and famines and plagues, so that the time of the promise arrives more quickly? A casual glance at a newspaper reminds us that that isn't necessary; it seems that disasters are happening regularly *enough* as all of creation groans for its redemption. Should we greet news of disasters as welcome acts of God? Jesus nowhere says that these things are by God's doing; from what we know of

God in *Jesus Christ*, it is much more likely that they are of the *devil* than that they are of God. Should we try to discern which calamities in our *own* time are jolting us toward the climax of history, and then go out on the street corners carrying placards saying, "The time is near!"? Jesus specifically instructs us not to make any assumptions about the imminence of the end; the end will come when we *least* expect it, even the most biblically astute. None of that is our business. *Our* business is to be faithful to Jesus Christ each day of our lives and in each circumstance of our lives, and so make our lives a continuous and unambiguous witness to God's love and mercy and trustworthiness. And the world being the way that it is, and people being the way that they are, we will likely find ourselves abandoned and betrayed and ridiculed because we *live* our faith as well as say the words, because we know that faith in Jesus Christ *cannot* be a *private* thing, because we take *seriously* Jesus' instruction to go out into the world and make disciples, because we have discovered that the only life worth *having* is the life that is ours in Jesus Christ. And so, threats to our reputation and our fortune are of far less concern to us than our commitment to being faithful. The temples that we have erected with our own hands and our own desires and our own imaginations are destined to come crashing down at our feet, and perhaps they must, in order to get us finally to rely upon God and upon God alone. When Jesus said, "You will be hated by all because of my name" (21:17), he was stating a simple fact; being faithful is not likely to make us the most popular people around. If that is what counts most for us, then we are in for some real bad news, every bit as awful as wars and earthquakes and famines and plagues. But here is the good news of the promise: "By your endurance you will gain your souls" (21:19).

The life of a disciple of Jesus Christ, after all is said and done, is not one of speculation or of judgmentalism—not even about the fact that *some* people seem to *deserve* being toasted worse than kippers and muffins. The life of a disciple is a life of behavior and dedication. Jesus has told us that, one day, there will be an *end* to life in the world as we know it. That news from a reliable source should be motive enough for us to keep our souls in shape for whatever is to come, unencumbered by the weight of whatever is excessive and useless and unworthy. The Lord is faithfully standing beside each of his faithful followers, giving us words and wisdom far beyond our personal ability and our native insight to cope with whatever natural disasters and human heartaches befall us, that in all things, we may give testimony to Jesus Christ. By our endurance, Luke the evangelist wanted us to know, we will gain our souls. And that *is* good news.

CHRIST THE KING SUNDAY

Spanish Springs Presbyterian Church, Sparks, Nevada

NOVEMBER 21, 2010

Jeremiah 23:1–6
Colossians 1:11–20
Luke 23:33–43

"The Kingdom Is Now"

My favorite author is the nineteenth-century English novelist Thomas Hardy. I enjoy the pictures of the English countryside and villages that he painted with words and his characterizations of simple people with their honest emotions. His books and stories are not happy tales. What he wrote were tragedies, really—in all of his great works, from *The Return of the Native* to *Jude the Obscure*, from *Tess of the D'Urbervilles* to *The Mayor of Casterbridge*, he told of basically good people who became victims of circumstance, of nature and of chance, of the blind and uncaring fate that Hardy believed dogs the human creature despite purity of heart and innocence of mind. Hardy's characters are Christian folk; the church and its rites are almost always a part of their days and seasons. But alongside their Christian faith, they had strong superstitions and prejudices, folkways and popular wisdom that had as much to do with guiding their thoughts and actions as did the Bible. Those of you who are familiar with Thomas Hardy will recognize what I mean.

    The epistle reading for this Christ the King Sunday strongly reminded me of the people in Hardy's novels and of Hardy's own fatalism. For it seems that the people of the Colossian church, though they had learned from the apostles the teachings of Jesus, actually lived as if faith in *him* were not enough for a successful life—that something more was required, that there were *other* powers than God the Father of Jesus Christ who had to be taken into account if one were to have salvation. They pictured a whole host of thrones and dominions and principalities and authorities holding sway over creation and over us human creatures, fates and spirits influencing our lives in good ways and bad, so that Jesus Christ crucified is not sufficient for our salvation. Instead, the Colossians assumed, we are held captive by invisible forces natural and *super*natural, a tyranny of darkness and secret magic that burdens the human spirit as it binds the human body.

The letter to the Colossians answered this by proclaiming that Christ is preeminent over all beings, and that in his crucifixion and resurrection, God has made us worthy to take the place reserved for us in the very presence of God. He has forgiven our sins and transformed our nature, not only *bestowing* upon us such an honor, but making us qualified to receive it. "He has rescued us from the power of darkness and transferred us into the kingdom of his beloved Son, in whom we have redemption, the forgiveness of sins" (Col 1:13).

It is easy to criticize the Colossians, like the characters of Thomas Hardy's stories, for their primitive mixture of Christianity with pagan superstitions of powers and spirits. But the more closely we look at their confused beliefs, the more we suspect that our *own* allegiances are not in proper order. For many of the rules by which *we* live are based on popular wisdom rather than the truth of Jesus Christ. Many of the standards by which we function are based on the conviction that there are forces and destinies and axioms of history and finance and politics and social intercourse which *should not* be *ignored* and *cannot* be *overridden*. We assume that we live in a time when it is not yet physically safe to turn the other cheek, when it is not yet socially prudent to give coat as well as cloak, when it is not yet hygienically wise to embrace the leper, all as Jesus taught and expected of his disciples, those who would be citizens of his kingdom. Jesus might have ridden into Jerusalem on a donkey to be put to death on a cross for our salvation, but surely *we* cannot be expected to make any sacrifices for *him*. Until we have saved up enough for our children and for our retirement, surely we cannot hazard giving our possessions to the poor. Until other nations become trustworthy, surely we cannot risk dismantling our nuclear weapons. Until the person who has wronged us has apologized, surely we cannot humiliate ourselves by forgiving him or her. In the future, perhaps, things might be different. We will continue to pray daily or weekly for the kingdom to come. But in the meantime, we know what must be done in order to survive in the world as it is, with its *other* dominions and powers and authorities and principalities. Jesus might have been the Son of God, but he was no realist. Jesus might be our king, but we will not surrender to him our common sense and our self-respect.

Indeed, it seems that most of us contemporary Christians—even or especially those in the denominations with the strictest congregational discipline—live *in spite of* rather than *in reliance upon* the proclamation that God has already delivered us from the power of darkness and transferred us into the kingdom of his beloved Son. Every bit as much as the Colossians, many contemporary Christians assume the validity of *lesser* powers and *inferior* truths and tend to place *their* authority above the teachings of *Christ*. Every bit as much as the Colossians, we find ourselves burdened in spirit and bound in body by the spells of political theories, by the charms of business savvy, and by the magic of self-interest. We seem to prefer the shadowy companionship of our familiar anxieties; we nurture the dark secrets in the recesses of our hearts rather than gamble on Christ's promise of new life; habits of fear and prejudice cause us to be suspicious of the kingship of Christ. Some of us are genuinely relieved, as we look around us, that Christ's reign seems so distant; citizenship in such a kingdom would be too radical a change from the way we have *been* thinking and behaving, too painful a departure from streetwise routines that have become so comfortable. Besides, what could Jesus have known of the practicalities of twenty-first-century life anyway? What could Christ know of the pressures of business and the seduction of credit cards and the demands of family and the threat of terrorism?

The ancient *Jews* long waited and watched and wondered when God would send the Messiah, the promised king of Israel descended from David, to establish his reign in Jerusalem and bring salvation. *Christians* have long waited and watched and wondered when *Christ's kingdom* would finally be established, and we would be free of the forces of hatred and fear and sin. When the Messiah finally did come to the Jews to establish his kingdom, he was rejected; most of them decided that *his* kingdom was not the sort that they really wanted. For all of our talk about the coming of Christ's kingdom, for all of our hymns and our prayers, many of us do not live as if we truly covet citizenship in it.

When Jesus entered Jerusalem, the prophecy of Zechariah was fulfilled. The religious leaders of the time, the scribes and Pharisees and Sadducees, detected in Jesus a threat to their revenues when he cleansed the temple and discerned in him a risk to the preeminence they enjoyed under Roman rule. They plotted against him and vigorously denied his claim to be king of the Jews. The Scottish biblical scholar W. M. MacGregor commented on John's version of Jesus' entry into Jerusalem,

> On this occasion Jesus did what He never did before or after. He was surrounded by [people] who talked and thought a great

deal about Messiah's coming, and who professed enthusiasm for it. The words were often on their lips; the hope, they said, was in their hearts; but Jesus, who knew the snare and the delusion of words, searched their profession to the bottom. . . . "You say you are looking for the Messiah's coming; you say that you look for Him to come to His capital riding on an ass; it has a good sound in the words of it, but here is the thing—such a King as the prophet spoke of—how do you like it now?" And what had seemed fascinating and credible, when it was found on the page of a sacred book, lost all its charm when it was seen in flesh.[1]

So we speak of Christ as the Prince of Peace, the friend of sinners, our eternal king. But the gospel of self-defense declares that we must meet force with force, and arm ourselves to destroy the entire planet many times over. Salvation by self-assertiveness directs that we push our own desires ahead of others' needs. Common sense dictates that we forbid children with AIDS from attending school with our kids. We say that it is unrealistic to turn the other cheek, to sell all that we have and give it to the poor, to visit the prisoner. In the meantime, some of us try to make Jesus Christ a capitalist or a socialist, a Democrat or a Republican, in hopes of legitimizing our own allegiance to ideologies and theories rather than to the gospel—Jesus Christ, for whom the universe was created and who is the goal toward which all of creation is tending, he who is the image of the invisible God, the first-born of all creation, he who is before all things and in whom all things hold together. "See to it," wrote the apostle to the Colossians, "that no one takes you captive through philosophy and empty deceit, according to human tradition, according to the elemental spirits of the universe, and not according to Christ" (Col 2:8). The thrones and dominions and principalities and authorities of our world call out their claims upon our loyalty as we approach the gates of the kingdom and peer inside, and many of us decide that it looked a lot better on paper, that it was more inviting when it was only a dream.

But scripture testifies that the kingdom is *not* merely a dream of what might be or a far-away hope that will come to pass in the sweet by and by. Christ already sits on his throne, and those who truly live by his teachings and submit fully to his sovereignty are already his subjects. Is Jesus Christ just one of *many* voices to which we should listen in life? Are the commands of Jesus Christ in the Bible simply *suggestions*, and *unrealistic* suggestions at that? Scripture rings with this truth: Jesus Christ is the Word of God, the perfect expression of God's love and God's will. Jesus Christ is the source,

---

1. W. M. MacGregor, *Jesus Christ, the Son of God* (Edinburgh: T. & T. Clark, 1907), quoted in Gossip, "St. John," 658.

channel, and goal of creation, God in direct relationship with the world. And we see life as it truly is *only* when we see it in relationship to him. Existence interpreted in any other way but as it relates to *Christ* is false—it's an illusion.

We are called to be citizens of the kingdom of Christ in every moment of our lives, and the kingdom is present in the midst of the world every time and every place that we acknowledge Christ as our king, taking seriously what he said and what he did, feeding the hungry, comforting the afflicted, unmasking pretention, befriending the forlorn, forgiving the sinner, welcoming the outcast, giving hospitality to the stranger. And that is the reality of God in Jesus Christ—we must not submit to the rule of hatred and fear and pride and envy and deceit and doubt, but we must bear witness to hope and compassion and kindness and generosity and justice and love. We must find our security not in superstitions and prejudices, folkways and popular wisdom, but solely in selfless obedience to our Lord. In a world where our enemies have the power to destroy us in a few seconds, in a culture devoted to profit and amusement, God has already delivered us from the power of darkness and transferred us into the kingdom of his beloved Son.

Who is your king? Are you living as a loyal subject of Jesus Christ, or do you still give your allegiance to thrones and dominions and principalities that have no power to redeem and no authority to forgive? Are you devoting your life to serving the first-born of creation, or are you hedging your bet by giving ear to other voices who would usurp the throne of Jesus Christ and postpone the advent of his kingdom? For the disciple of Jesus Christ, the kingdom is not something for which we must watch and wait and wonder. For the disciple of Jesus Christ, the kingdom is now.

Evening before the National Day
of Thanksgiving

Spanish Springs Presbyterian Church, Sparks, Nevada
November 24, 2010

Deuteronomy 8:1–10
1 Timothy 2:1–7
Matthew 6:25–33

"Life as Thanksgiving"

There is a saying commonly but probably mistakenly attributed to the fourteenth-century Christian mystic and scholar Meister Eckhart: "If the only prayer you ever said was 'Thanks', it would be enough." That may seem like a strange bit of wisdom from a person who was assumed to be in frequent and intimate connection with God, someone whom we might suppose spent many hours each day in prayer about a whole host of topics. Some people, of course, never get even *that* far in conversation with God—saying "Thanks." And the fact that worship services at Thanksgiving-time in America are dwindling in number and in attendance suggests that the world's disinclination to credit God with being the source of human prosperity and achievement has spread even to the Christian church. It isn't that we don't pray, we modern Christians. But much of the time, we are so busy asking God for *more* that we lose sight of the abundance that we already *have*. And when *that* happens, we tend to become *anxious* about our life—whether we will have it *tomorrow*. And, of course, that was what Jesus identified as the preoccupation of the Gentiles, meaning, in that context, all those people who did not believe in the God of Israel.

For Jesus himself, the Gospels make it clear that prayer was an indispensable part of his daily life. And among the subjects of his prayer was giving thanks to God, including even on the occasion of what he knew would be his last meal with his disciples before his death on the cross—a feature that is, or should be, a part of our *own* practice of the Lord's Supper, the sacrament universally known, throughout the church, as the eucharist, which is the Greek word for "thanksgiving." It seems very strange, then, that, when his own disciples asked that he teach them how to pray, Jesus taught them a form of prayer that includes not a single explicit word of thanksgiving in it. It speaks of dearness and intimacy: "Our Father." It speaks of God's divine sovereignty: "who art in heaven." It speaks of God's untouchable holiness: "Hallowed be thy name." It speaks of the superiority of God's intention and the certainty of God's future: "Thy kingdom come. Thy will be done." It speaks of the shortcomings of human behavior when it requests that God's goal be fulfilled "On earth as it is in heaven"—an admission that history is still short of its destiny. It confidently petitions God for that which we need in life, and so confirms that God is the dependable source of our necessities: "Give us this day our daily bread." It makes a claim on God's mercy, testifying that God's compassion has never failed and that it is the pattern for our dealings with one another: "And forgive us our debts, as we also have forgiven our debtors." And it acknowledges God's power to preserve our lives from destruction: "And lead us not into temptation, [b]ut deliver us from evil" (Matt 6:9–13 RSV). But the Lord's Prayer includes not a *word* of what Eckhart is quoted as saying was the one *necessary* subject of our communication with God, and what many a Sunday school teacher has taught is the most important.

I think, perhaps, the Lord's Prayer does not specifically include words of thanksgiving for the simple fact that thanksgiving ought not to be confined to the words of a prayer, even a prayer offered daily, but finds its best and truest and most sincere expression in our deeds and actions. Many parents have known the frustration of having taught a child to say the words "Thank you," only to have them repeated mechanically and apparently without any real sense of gratitude; learning the words alone doesn't mean that there is any attitude of thanksgiving behind them. The real test of whether someone is thankful or not is better gauged in their behavior. So, the most important activity in life—worship—is, if it is genuine, intrinsically motivated by thanksgiving. Our occupations, if conducted with honesty and to the best of our ability, are expressions of gratitude for the means and opportunity to contribute back to the Creator in gratitude for the creative faculties with which we have been endowed; then, we come to regard our livelihoods as *vocations*. Our spending habits are one of the most accurate measures of whether we are truly grateful for God's blessings. It is when we *ourselves* give away freely that we are best acknowledging that what *we* have has been given freely to *us*, and not something that we think we have created by ourselves and thus must jealously guard against loss or theft.

The portion of the Sermon on the Mount that we have as our Gospel reading this evening lies close to the very heart of Jesus' teaching. *True life*—life with the quality of the *eternal*—is possible *only* when we receive life as a *gift*, for only when life is received as a *gift*, rather than thought of as something that must be *earned* and *clung* to, *safeguarded* and *rationed*, can it be lived with genuine confidence and without reserve. A life that is all wrapped up in itself, in constant concern for its own welfare and habitually measuring itself to make sure that nothing is missing, is life lived with suspicion, with fear, without any sense of wonder and without any welcome of surprise.

On some occasions, Jesus was critical of people who had many possessions. We remember his words to the rich young man who offered to follow Jesus but was reluctant to give up what he owned in order to be free to go wherever Jesus would lead him. We recall Jesus' parable about the man who decided to tear down his barns to build bigger ones in order to hold his bumper crop. God called him a fool. Just a couple of weeks ago, we heard again how Jesus was much more impressed with the poor widow who put into the temple treasury two copper coins—all that she owned—than he was with the wealthy who contributed a lot more, but less than their entire fortune. It would be tempting to picture as Jesus' audience on the mountainside a crowd of wealthy people who employed accountants and managers to make sure that they not only *got* wealthy and *stayed* wealthy, but got wealthier *still*. Much more likely, the people who were free to follow Jesus out into the fields and onto the hillsides were poorer folk, for whom concern about food and clothing was urgent—not so much a matter of *what* to eat and *what* to wear, but whether they would be *able* to eat and whether they would have anything at *all* to protect them against the cold. It wasn't to the well-fed and well-dressed that Jesus spoke these words, probably, but to people many of whom *already* lived off of scraps and wore hand-me-downs. "'You cannot serve God and wealth'" (6:24c), he had just told them. And many of them, we can imagine, dreamed of wealth, of being able to afford whatever they desired. "'Therefore I tell you, do not worry about your life, what you will eat or what you will drink, or about your body, what you will wear. Is not life *more* than food, and the body *more* than clothing?'" (6:25). Well, yes, they might have answered, but it's not like these other things aren't important.

To which Jesus would surely have agreed. His point wasn't that we don't need food or clothes. His point was being so grateful for God's very gift of life that we live out our gratitude in trust of God's continuing providence, including in our actions and attitudes toward others. God has given us breath and body. God is not wasteful. God will provide what is necessary for whatever God has made, as even nature teaches us. "'Look at the birds of the air; they neither sow nor reap nor gather into barns, and yet your heavenly Father feeds them. Are you not of more value than they?'" (6:25–26). God has invested in us a bit of God himself—God's very own image; God will not let that precious investment languish or dwindle. Besides, it is not our own efforts that create life, and it is not our own anxiety about tomorrow that causes the sun to rise. "'Can any of you by worrying add a single hour to your span of life? And why do you worry about clothing? Consider the lilies of the field, how they grow; they neither toil nor spin, yet I tell you, even Solomon in all his glory was not clothed like one of these. But if God so clothes the grass of the field, which is alive today and tomorrow is thrown into the oven, will he not much more clothe you—you of little faith?'" (6:27–30).

We are not showing gratitude for what we have been given *today* if we are fretting about whether the giver will be similarly generous *tomorrow*. What would you think of a child whose first words upon receiving a birthday present were, "So what are you going to give me next year?" Even if such a rude question were preceded by the word "thanks," the gratitude would seem pretty shallow. "'Therefore do not worry, saying, "What will we eat?" or "What will we drink?" or "What will we wear?" For it is the Gentiles'"—those who don't *believe* in the God who was faithful to Abraham and Isaac and Jacob and in whom you say *you* believe—"'For it is the Gentiles who strive for all these things'" (6:31–32a)—who think that life is all about the sort of wealth and possessions that fill cupboards and closets and storage units. The God who was generous enough to give us life and provide for today knows what we need tomorrow. "'But strive first for the kingdom of God and his righteousness, and all these things will be given to you as well'" (6:33).

Perhaps it is not your habit to read or think about that passage as a call to gratitude. Like the Lord's Prayer, it says nothing specifically about being thankful. But do you see that profound thankfulness is what stands behind the proper attitude about all of these things?—how anxiety and covetousness about what we do *not* have, or do not *yet* have, is really something of an *insult* to the Giver, as if a child were to look at all the opened gifts under the Christmas tree, and say, "But why didn't you give me such-and-such as well?"

It is hard, virtually impossible, to be thankful when we're busy trying to glut ourselves on things that we fancy, or to secure ourselves against every contingency. It was hard for people in Jesus' day, before retirement plans and insurance and all the other devices by which we try to make our own future and call it simple "prudence." How much harder today, with advertising to stimulate our acquisitiveness and stoke our greed and fuel our anxieties, and when even what is regarded in some places as worship seems to be about how we can get healthier and wealthier by winning God's favor? Maybe our worship should routinely include a time of prayer in which we simply say the two words "thank you," and allow the silence afterward to shout an emphatic exclamation point that prompts an entire week of generosity, of forgiveness, of kindness, of forbearance, of joy.

Life lived as one continuous expression of thanksgiving is much more convincing a sign of real gratitude toward God than an endless tumble of words. Perhaps Jesus took for granted that his disciples, asking him how they should pray, would already be taking care of the "thank you" part in all the rest of life. The parent, too, knows that there is finally understanding behind the child's words of thanks when the child, in turn, is eager to give to another. And we can be gratified to know that our children's generosity has come about because they have learned to trust that their own parents' generosity with the necessities in their life—food and clothing and such—hasn't stopped, but will be dependable tomorrow and the next day.

Are you thankful enough to God for what God has freely given you to be generous, forgiving, kind, forbearing, and joyful yourself?—to allow all of life to be an expression of your gratitude, trusting in the dependable love and provision of God? It might be, as the saying goes, that "if the only prayer you ever said was 'Thanks', it would be enough." But the far more meaningful way for us to express our gratitude to God is to live free of anxiety and preoccupation about ourselves and full of generosity and compassion for others.

Appendix

The first of the three sermons in this appendix was preached during a service of morning prayer on the first anniversary of the attacks upon the World Trade Center and the Pentagon and the heroic thwarting of an attempt to destroy the United States Capitol, and is based on the scripture readings for the day in Year 2 of the two-year Daily Lectionary cycle. As so often happens, the Daily Lectionary spoke well to the special need of the occasion. In the days immediately following the September 11 horrors, we had offered a special worship service that was attended by neighbors of our storefront church facility as well as members of the Spanish Springs Presbyterian congregation who felt the need to gather to raise our voices and open our hearts to God in the midst of fear and sadness and dismay and anger and confusion. The gathering on September 11, 2002, came after a year of highly charged public rhetoric, vows of vengeance, disinclination toward communal self-examination, and preparation for a war whose repercussions continue to shake the national and international social, political, and moral landscape.

The second sermon offers an additional perspective on the scripture readings for the Twentieth Sunday in Ordinary Time during Year C of the Common Lectionary (Revised). The subject matter—addressing a verse of scripture upon which I have never heard homiletical reflection—seemed important enough to supplement the sermon that appears in the main text.

The final sermon was written at the request of the Nevada Interfaith Council for Worker Justice, of which I was a part, as a sample sermon addressing, from a Christian biblical perspective, the importance of adequate communal support for government services, specifically the appropriateness of a progressive state income tax as the fairest way to meet the needs of all state residents. Nevada has famously long been without a state income tax, historically relying on income from steady or declining gaming and mineral extraction to pay for government services, but more and more necessitating increases in sales taxes and fees that fall hardest on those least able to shoulder the burden. In the second decade of the twenty-first century, there was increasing debate about the merits of instituting a progressive income tax as the most appropriate means of financing state infrastructure and social services—a position advocated by the Council, whose mission was to offer a Christian witness in support of laboring people and the poor much in the spirit of similar organizations that expressed Christian concern for the well-being of the working class and unemployed a century earlier.

Morning Prayer

Spanish Springs Presbyterian Church, Sparks, Nevada
September 11, 2002

Job 29:1–6; 30:1–2, 16–31
Acts 14:19–28
John 11:1–16

Sitting on a pile of ashes, enveloped in a cloud of dust, Job longed for things to be like they had once been—prosperous, untroubled, secure. He had scarcely been conscious of what grief was, life for him had been so perfect. But now his life had come tumbling in on him. His self-assurance had collapsed into a heap of rubble as he lost his home, his family, his servants (his "company," if you will), his health. Everything that he had counted on as security in the world, everything that was comfortable and familiar, everything that gave him pride of being and a sense of accomplishment, had been taken away unexpectedly and through no fault of his own. His friends told him that it was judgment for some sin he would not confess, but he knew himself to be blameless, and that made his disaster even more poignant. He had done nothing to deserve his pain and suffering, so he began to sense that he had been abandoned by God.

> "Oh, that I were as in the months of old,
>   as in the days when God watched over me" [he lamented;]
> "when his lamp shone over my head,
>   and by his light I walked through darkness;
> when I was in my prime,
>   when the friendship of God was upon my tent;
> when the Almighty was still with me,
>   when my children were around me;
> when my steps were washed with milk,
>   and the rock poured out for me streams of oil!" (Job 29:2–6)

In other words, when the world was his oyster, when the world's troubles were distant, when his enemies, if he had any, had no power over him. In a series of quick disasters, it had all been taken away from him, leaving him to survey the destruction around him, hardly able to comprehend it, scarcely able to believe it was happening to him.

> "And now my soul is poured out within me;
> days of affliction have taken hold of me....
> He has cast me into the mire,
> and I have become like dust and ashes." (30:16, 19)

And some of his neighbors scoffed at him.

Job was dismayed that God would let this all happen to him. His life, as well as he knew it, had been all virtue. He never thought he would stand in the same shoes as people whose wickedness earned them God's wrath and the devil's destruction. For the first time in his life, he knew what so many other people experienced in their lives—tragedies, he might have assumed, that were the result of their own sins and omissions. He probably supposed, like many of us, that people make their own luck, good or bad. For the first time in his life, his self-assurance was stripped away to reveal his ultimate and utter dependence upon God. And he feared, because of his suffering, that God no longer cared for him. In the everyday routine of planting and harvesting, he might not have thought much about the one who really gives the growth. Job's calamity nearly broke him. But amid the dust and the ashes, he came to realize that God still watched over him and came to understand who God the Creator is, and who Job the creature was, and, perhaps, to have a new compassion for those around him who had been suffering pain and loss while he prospered.

In a depth of wisdom that is unfathomable to mortals like you and me, God has chosen not to exclude evil from the world that God created and called good. God ordained the cycle of birth and death as a part of the world's goodness; the Bible does not teach that God ever intended us creatures to have bodies that do not age and eventually die. Most of us, though not all of us, come to terms with our mortality. What most of us cannot come to terms with, nor should we ever accept as a natural part of existence, are cruelty, hatred, violence of deed or violence of thought. Most of us could not conceive of the enormity of the active evil that worked a sudden Armageddon in New York, in Washington, in rural Pennsylvania, though we had heard about Auschwitz, about Lockerbie, about Beirut, about Srebrenica, about My Lai.

The God who raised Jesus Christ from the tomb is the God who is able to work miracles of redemption from every hopeless scenario, as Jesus himself raised Lazarus from the dead. Families and friends and congregations and communities have committed the souls of those who perished on September 11—office workers, passengers, messengers, executives, flight crews, shop keepers, janitors, police officers, fire fighters; mothers, fathers, children, grandparents, lovers, colleagues, friends—to the eternal care of God. We remember them this day, we reassert our trust in God, we ask again God's blessing upon our nation, we rededicate ourselves to justice and liberty, and, I hope, we pray for peace. And we offer ourselves as instruments for God's use in working a miracle of wholeness and redemption that will transform seeming unmitigated disaster into a dawn of new gratitude for life, new appreciation for each other as contributors to a society of righteousness and fairness and dignity for all, new reverence toward God, the creator and sustainer of all life, new obedience to God's command to love our neighbor as ourselves, recognizing each person, even the lowliest, as our neighbor.

As nations rattle their swords, we need to ponder the grief that we experienced when hatred too familiar to the rest of the world touched our shores, and pledge ourselves not to be a part of anyone else's similar misery. As this plan and that for regimes of security are proposed and purchased and then circumvented, we need to turn again to the only true security that any of us has in this life—faith in the loving and dependable promises of God. As newspapers once again find room for stories of famine and disease and oppression, we need to get on with the daily duty of loving our neighbors on this shrinking planet, which means doing deeds of justice and kindness and generosity and mercy.

In the dust and ashes of his incredible loss, all the work of a powerful force opposed to the will of God, Job discovered a joy more profound than his leisure, discovered a security more dependable than his possessions, discovered a comfort more genuine than the wisdom of his culture. He discovered life's only true strength, life's only true satisfaction, life's only true hope. He discovered God, who raised him from the ash heap and breathed into him new life—life lived in proper relationship to God and, therefore, proper relationship to those around him. May such a discovery, such a life, such a relationship, be the enduring legacy of the ash and dust of September 11, 2001—a dawn of new commitment for America, and a dawn of new hope for humankind.

Twentieth Sunday in Ordinary Time

Spanish Springs Presbyterian Church, Sparks, Nevada

August 15, 2010

Isaiah 5:1–7
Hebrews 11:29—12:2
Luke 12:49-56

"Keeping Faith"

It's not unusual for us to hear people say that we owe something to the generations that will come after us. Many of the decisions that you and I make now will affect our children and our grandchildren and our great-grandchildren, both in ways that we can fairly well forecast and in ways that we haven't even dreamed of. Certainly, we know this is true of the environment—look at how people are being affected today by the decision of earlier generations to depend upon fossil fuels as our primary energy source and to rely on the internal combustion engine for our transportation. We know it is true of the economy—the debts incurred under administrations both Republican and Democratic will long have an effect on our nation's quality of life, but so do decisions about regulation and de-regulation, for instance. Legal decisions handed down today become precedent that guides future judges, for good or ill, until some high court breaks precedent, but even then the course of individual lives and perhaps our entire society will have been altered, sometimes, perhaps, in ways that are quite tragic. Yes, we do owe something to the generations that will come after us—generations that we will have brought into being.

    Less often do we hear people say that we have obligations to the generations that preceded us. But how can that be—that we should have any responsibilities toward people who died before we were even born? How can someone in the past—the recent past or distant antiquity—be affected by what you or I do today? Oh, we might sometimes hear that we mustn't squander the fruits of sacrifices that have been made by our predecessors—for instance, that we should honor with our vigilance today the liberty that our American forebears fought and sometimes died for, or that we should honor with our own hard work the foundation that has been laid for us by our parents, or that we should respect by our own dedication those who pioneered some organization to which we belong or the company by which we are employed. But, in those cases, we don't suppose that our own faithfulness to principle or to hard work or to military service really has a direct benefit to anyone who is already in his or her grave.

In the eleventh chapter of the writing that we know as the letter to the Hebrews, we are told, "Now faith is the assurance of things hoped for, the conviction of things not seen. Indeed, by faith our ancestors received approval" (Heb 11:1–2). And then there is a long list of the great personages of the Old Testament and the many instances in which they acted in decisive ways based not on tangible evidence of some immediate and personal gain, but in reliance on God to fulfill the divine promises, perhaps beyond their own lifetime and in ways that they could not foresee. And then there is this curious statement at the end of the chapter, a portion of our reading this morning: "Yet all these, though they were commended for their faith, did not receive what was promised, since God had provided something better so that they would not, apart from us, be made perfect" (11:39–40). Did that get your attention when you first heard it? ". . . so that they would not, apart from us, be made perfect" (11:40b). Were you aware that the "perfection" of Abel, Noah, Abraham, Isaac, Jacob, Joseph, Moses, Gideon, Barak, Samson, Jephthah, David, Samuel, the prophets, and many others is in some real way dependent upon you, and your faith? That's what Hebrews seems to say—"so that they"—all those great people of the Bible—"would not, apart from us, be made perfect" (11:40b).

"Perfect," in the Bible, means "complete," "finished," "fulfilled," "not lacking anything." It is not so much a matter of moral flawlessness. Only God and Christ are perfect in that sense, and the Bible would never be so sacrilegious as to suggest that any created human being could be as morally pure as Jesus. God's flawlessness, demonstrated in the life of Jesus, might be our standard for behavior—indeed, it should be—but there is no suggestion that we can attain it. Hebrews elsewhere acknowledges that only Jesus, although tempted, remained without sin. In Hebrews, as in most of the Bible, "perfection" refers to more than moral goodness. (Although Jesus was "holy, blameless, undefiled" and "separated from sinners," nevertheless, according to Hebrews, he still had to become "perfect"—had to be fully obedient, as well as fully qualified for the task before him.) The perfection of the faithful people who came before us—their fulfillment, their completion, their no longer lacking in anything—depends, Hebrews says, on *our* being faithful. And so, the Bible is telling us, we have an obligation toward all the many earlier generations of people who set aside, deferred, risked, and endured in faith that God would be faithful to the promises he made to all with whom he covenanted to be their God.

Wait a minute, you might be saying to yourself. I don't remember agreeing to any such thing when I became a church member, or even before that, when I was baptized. I have quite enough responsibility caring for myself and my family, planning ahead and scrimping to provide something for my grandchildren, perhaps, or provide for the welfare of the people I employ. But how can I possibly be held responsible for the well-being of my own ancestors, much less people thousands of years ago who have no connection to my family tree?

We live in a regrettably a-historical age. There have always been people who live only in the moment, who are oblivious to how we got where we are, individually and as a society, who think that the world began when they were born and, as far as they are concerned, will end when they die, and in the meantime has no existence beyond the limit of their own rather narrow field of vision. Jay Leno has a feature on his program occasionally where he interviews people on the street, asking them if they recognize names or dates or events from history and even from current headlines. It is mildly amusing, but profoundly troubling, how many people have no idea what he is talking about. Perhaps my concern runs a little deeper because of having been trained as an historian, but I really think that we should all be alarmed at the corporate loss of memory in our society—and the "What does it mean to me?" attitude of so many people, young and old. And as people of God, it is especially crucial to remember, to perceive, and to be thankful. Worship of God, offering to God, heeding God, are all based on being thankful to God, and being thankful to God depends upon remembering God's faithful goodness.

That's largely the point of the Bible. Scripture testifies that God acts in, through, and over time. In the words and deeds of people who honor God's purpose and follow God's ways, God's persistent goal of restoring creation to the loving harmony and communion that God always intended is coming ever more near. At times, God's people have suffered persecution and torment in a world that stubbornly resists the purpose for which God brought it into being, but the purpose remains valid and God's promise remains true. And, at the pivot point of history, God himself appeared on the calendar in human form, living and working in the minutes and hours and days and years of a carpenter's son, a teacher, a healer, a messenger of hope and proclaimer of forgiveness, turning many to the truth of God's sovereignty but rejected by some, and then being put to death by those who themselves wanted to have control of history. But then the reality of Jesus' identity and the truth of his teaching and the steadfastness of his love were made manifest when he was raised from the tomb and appeared, still bearing the marks of his torture, to those who believed in him. He had been born into this world at a particular place on a particular date. He was executed at a particular place on a particular date, about thirty-three years later. And on the third day after that, after the tomb was discovered to be empty, he was present again for a time in visible form among his friends.

You and I would not know any of that were it not for the faithful witness of the many generations before us, and the church, the vessel in which the precious treasure of the gospel has been preserved and transmitted, has been demonstrated and testified to, all these many centuries. We are heirs of a faith shaped and articulated and made dear by the blood of martyrs, and by the selfless sacrifices of countless believers, and by the day-in, day-out confident and obedient and hopeful words and deeds of people not so very different from you and me. But we have not yet arrived at the finish line of faith's race. The goal remains still ahead in the final consummation of all things with the return and the unrivaled lordship of Christ. And each link in the chain of faithfulness stretching from Abel, who was the first one to make an offering that was pleasing to the Lord, to the glorious day of God's final triumph over all the powers that stand in the way of the world's full redemption, is vital and necessary if the witness of any one of God's people is to be of lasting significance. Our faithfulness will hasten the day of God's consummation of history. Our unfaithfulness will retard its arrival and the final resurrection to eternal life.

Yes, we owe it to those who came before us, who toiled and sacrificed and resisted temptation and refused to give in to discouragement and persecution and anxiety and fear, to keep faith, so that theirs may come to perfection—completion, fulfillment, not lacking anything—that great cloud of witnesses without whom you and I would not know about the love and mercy and salvation of God, would not know the words and deeds and continuing presence of Jesus Christ his Son, would not know the strength and joy and gifts of the Holy Spirit. Each generation owes it to all the generations to come to proclaim and demonstrate the faith and to nurture its development in young and old alike. But each generation also owes it to all the generations that came before it to be faithful in turn so that their striving toward the kingdom of God will not be unappreciated and their march interrupted by a generation that turns away from the goal by deciding that it can manufacture its own destiny or that it can invent its own salvation or that it can refashion God to suit its own definition of paradise or, perhaps, by thinking and acting as if today is all that matters, my wants and my life, and that all this talk about a God is irrelevant to me, if not total nonsense. And the chain would be broken. And the Creator's goal for all creation would go unannounced. And all the sacrifices made and the witness given and the prayers voiced by countless faithful in the past—what meaning would they have? And the death and resurrection of Jesus Christ—what point would there be, without a present generation of believers to proclaim it and give witness to it in their lives, and to give substance to the faithfulness that steadfastly hoped in God's promise of a Messiah?

Not a single generation has yet lived to see the promise of God's will of redemption fulfilled, completed, made perfect—to see the final consummation of history. But each generation of faithful believers has been able to testify—and has done so—from its own experience understood in the light of scripture and with the vibrant sense of Christ's continuing life within and among them and the power of the Holy Spirit at work in their midst, that God's purpose is being fulfilled, is nearing completion, is tending toward perfection, that the goodness of God to which previous generations gave their own witness continues, and that therefore all God's promises of a new creation will be fulfilled as well. And you and I who have been blessed to know of God in Christ and to understand God's faithfulness through the lens of Christ's resurrection and to experience the gift of the Holy Spirit in our lives and in the life of Christ's church add, with every faithful word and deed, a new level of hopefulness to the foundation laid by the faithful whose words and deeds are recorded in the Bible. Our faithfulness today is a necessary step in their perfection. Our witness today is an essential link in the chain that stretches the ancient hope toward the future consummation and makes every instance of our forebears' suffering or sacrifice for the sake of the gospel a blessing to you and to me and enfolds us into that great cloud of witnesses.

Nevada Interfaith Council for Worker Justice

Exodus 33:12–23
Romans 13:1–7
Matthew 22:15–22

"The Things That Are God's"

One day, when Jesus was approached by some people who were more interested in complaining about him than actually having their question answered, Jesus responded to their interrogation with one of his few statements regarding something that a lot of people (including a lot of modern Americans, and including many people of faith) regard as a nasty subject—taxes. "'Tell us, then, what you think,'" Jesus' enemies said to him. "'Is it lawful to pay taxes to the emperor, or not?'" (Matt 22:17)—"Should we pay them, or should we not?" Jesus' answer is famous, though it doesn't seem to stop anyone's grumbling about payments to the government. "'Give . . . to the emperor the things that are the emperor's,'" he said, "'and to God the things that are God's'" (22:21b). Jesus' antagonists, we are told, were utterly amazed at him—not only because the shrewdness of his answer provided no grounds on which to have him arrested, but also, perhaps, because he offered them no argument against what they considered an unpleasant chore—paying taxes!

The Pharisees, who only asked their question in order to entrap Jesus, were popular with the people in part because they resented and complained about paying taxes to the Roman regime. Others, nationalists and zealots, publicly refused to pay taxes; their objections were not about paying taxes per se so much as paying taxes to a pagan occupier of the land God had given to the descendants of Abraham, and of whom God was the ultimate ruler. Whether they would have supported a general tax revolt against an Israelite king, we don't know. They specifically were opposed to the "census"—a head-tax imposed by Rome upon the inhabitants of Judea when they made it a Roman province, during Jesus' childhood. The tax could be paid only with Roman coins, and Roman coins bore an inscription that many Jews considered to be blasphemy, to the effect that Emperor Tiberius was the son of Augustus, who had been declared to be a god. If Jesus had answered "Yes" to the Pharisees' question, he would have been regarded as a friend of the Romans and an enemy of the Jews. If Jesus had answered "No" to their question, he would have been liable to arrest by the Romans as an insurrectionist, encouraging others to violate the law.

Curiously, when Jesus asked to see one of the idolatrous coins by which the tax could be paid, the Pharisees had one handy, even though they were within the sacred precincts of the temple—a place where anything considered unclean was forbidden. "'Whose head is this, and whose title?'" (22:20) Jesus asked them as they held it out to him. "'The emperor's'" (22:21a), they responded. He then told them to give to the emperor what was already his—the money that the emperor had issued, which bore the emperor's marks of ownership, and which would satisfy the emperor's demands.

Already, the Pharisees were accomplices in the emperor's economic and political system. They benefited from it in various ways, traveling the emperor's roads, relying on the emperor's protection, using goods that came through the emperor's seaports. And they traded in the emperor's currency. (They even had some of it in their pocketbooks there on the holy ground of the temple!) Paying taxes to support the secular state, even a pagan state, is not an offense to God. It is through such instruments as emperors that God's purpose is achieved, even if they do not intend for their decrees and conquests to be part of God's great drama of redemption. God remains sovereign over the kings and presidents and prime ministers and governors of this world, whether they know it or not, whether they acknowledge God's sovereignty or not. Even something as earthy as taxes can serve a divine plan. But aside from the emperor's philosophy about whether he was an instrument of God, he commanded that the people of Judea pay to support the government. Taxes, Jesus apparently recognized, are a fact of life in society.

This brings us to the real issue about taxes. They are the way that a society provides those things that the society has decided are important for the common well-being. Sometimes, the common well-being calls for expenditures for services that virtually everyone uses all the time, like roads and waterworks. Sometimes, the common well-being calls for expenditures for services that directly affect only a few, but which society at large regards as beneficial to the whole community because the needs of the few are being served, like schools for children and health care for the elderly poor. Some societies may decide that the whole community would benefit from broadening the government's provision of such services, like making health care universally available to all, either on the grounds that it is a basic task of government or simply because the society's prosperity makes it possible, or that schools should be available for higher education and even adult re-training as the workplace changes and new information and skills need to be learned by some for the benefit of the whole. The specifics are matters for the political system to determine; Jesus did not get into a discussion about how much tax should be collected and what services it should fund. The point is that no society can exist without some contribution from individuals to provide for shared needs. Indeed, that is one functional definition of a "society." And the way societies have long done that is by the levy and collection of taxes.

Much as a lot of us, from time to time, would like to find an island somewhere and cut ourselves off from the rest of the world and be responsible only for our own survival, Jesus and the prophets before him didn't know of any such lifestyle. Even periodic retreat into prayer and contemplation was for the purpose of renewal to serve others. The faith of Abraham was a trustful obedience that sprung from a promise of a nation that would be a blessing to all other nations. The faith of Abraham that has been passed down to Jews and Muslims and Christians is intensely social—it is based on reciprocal obligations and loyalties between God and the believer that are fulfilled and satisfied only as believers interact with other human beings. The scriptures were written to form and bind communities of people and, in part, to teach them how to live together in joy and gratitude and justice, certainly not to drive them apart in suspicion or greed or jealousy. The law of Moses is about relationships. The precepts of the Qur'an are about relationships. The teachings of Jesus are about relationships. And relationships involve responsibility for other people, promoting the well-being of other people, serving other people.

Believers in the God who created the world and everything in it, who testify to the command to be fruitful and multiply, who acknowledge that we are to be helpers of one another, know that we are our brother's keeper (and our sister's keeper, too), that we do not live in isolation and cannot escape the responsibilities of stewardship of the earth's resources and the societies they support, that God promises sufficiency for all our needs when the earth's resources are distributed fairly and used for wholesome purposes. That does not make every public payment good. That does not make every public expenditure wise. But it does make every Jew, Christian, and Muslim accountable as members of the social fabric into which God has woven you, me, and everyone else. It should make paying taxes less a matter of grudging necessity and more a matter of communal stewardship. And it poses a serious ethical question for individuals and corporations that would seek to evade payment of taxes, whether it be by disguising assets or mischaracterizing transactions or by divorcing and remarrying to qualify for a lower tax rate or by opening a sham office on foreign soil. Private individuals' cleverness and corporate directors' schemes make interesting headlines. But greed is never a worthy motive, and greed that has the effect of robbing from the fund that supports the common well-being, especially in a society that defines the public well-being by democratic process, is a reason for shame, not admiration.

The apostle Paul, writing to citizens of the city of Rome who had turned away from pagan idols to the God of Abraham and Sarah, commanded his readers to subject themselves to the governing authorities,

> for there is no authority except from God, and those authorities that exist have been instituted by God. Therefore whoever resists authority resists what God has appointed, and those who resist will incur judgment. For rulers are not a terror to good conduct, but to bad. Do you wish to have no fear of the authority? Then do what is good. . . . For the same reason you also pay taxes, for the authorities are God's servants, busy with this very thing. Pay to all what is due them—taxes to whom taxes are due, revenue to whom revenue is due, respect to whom respect is due, honor to whom honor is due. (Rom 13:1b–3b, 6–7)

Specifically, Paul was reminding his Christian audience that living in anticipation of the kingdom of God does not exempt anyone from fulfilling our responsibilities in the kingdoms of the world, and that, so far as it does not involve immorality or harm to others, being a good Christian means being a good citizen. Centuries later, commenting on Paul's admonition to the Christians at Rome, John Calvin declared that we cannot resist the magistrate without resisting God at the same time. "With hearts inclined to reverence their rules, the subjects should prove their obedience toward them, whether by obeying their proclamations, or by paying taxes, or by undertaking public offices and burdens which pertain to the common defense, or by executing any other commands of theirs."[1]

If people of faith have the obligation to support the well-being of society, and if the common method of doing so is by paying lawful taxes, it follows that the taxes should be adequate to meet the public needs. If the existing taxes are not meeting the public needs, people of faith should be involved in advocating a system of taxation at rates that will, always exercising

---

1. Calvin, *Institutes of the Christian Religion*, IV.XX.23, in McNeill, 1510. Regarding wastefulness of taxes, see IV.XX.13, in McNeill, 1501–2, including n33.

care that those least able to pay are not unfairly burdened or left unable to meet the basic needs of their own household. The prophets declare, with virtual unanimity, God's concern that the poor not be further impoverished by rulers' edicts and society's disregard.

In the name of "fairness," some people today advocate more reliance upon sales taxes and less on income taxes. The effect of that, however, would be to do the very thing the prophets condemn—sales taxes fall heaviest on those who already are unable to afford anything more than the bare necessities of life. Progressive taxes on the income of individuals and corporations impose the greatest tax burden upon those who are in the best position to pay it and who have materially benefited the most from the services, privileges, and protections afforded by government. People of faith do not look for ways they can give away less of what God has entrusted to them to be used as a blessing for all. People of faith recognize that they are stewards of the gifts God has bestowed, and that, the greater the gift, the greater the obligation to apply it for the benefit of all.

In a perfect world, perhaps, there would be no need for taxes; people would be alert to recognize needs and respond to them generously without a tax ever being levied. In a democratic republic, we have the privilege of electing legislators and governors to assess the public well-being and to determine how it will best be achieved. In that process, the advocacy and scrutiny of individuals and organizations that have discerned unmet needs and, yes, waste of public funds, is critical. In a democracy, the responsibility of people of faith in the God from whom all blessings flow and from whom all human rights derive is greater even than in the kingdoms of old. And, perhaps, the judgment upon our failures to do so will be more severe. Whether the Pharisees who sought to entrap Jesus afterward paid their taxes more cheerfully is doubtful. But that episode teaches, among other things, that earthly government has a positive role in God's scheme for humankind, and that people of faith have no theological rationale for opposing its work, and a strong, faith-centered rationale for supporting it and improving it. Whatever sacrifices we make to honor God are of no account if the poor and the oppressed, the disadvantaged and the powerless, are being ignored. Lavish praise offered to God in the temple is drowned out in God's ears by the cries of the needy in the streets. It is sometimes by giving to the emperor the things that are the emperor's that God's purpose is achieved.

A lot of people have never seen a tax that they liked. But God has never seen a social need that God could forget. "Pay to all what is due them—taxes to whom taxes are due, revenue to whom revenue is due, respect to whom respect is due, honor to whom honor is due" (Rom 13:7). "Give therefore to the emperor the things that are the emperor's, and to God the things that are God's" (Matt 22:21b).

List of Sources Cited

Askey, David, dir. "Fire and Brimstone." *Bless Me, Father*. Aired July 26, 1981.
Bonhoeffer, Dietrich. *Ethics*. Edited by Eberhard Bethge. Translated by Neville Horton Smith. New York: Macmillan, 1955.
Dawn, Marva J. *Keeping the Sabbath Wholly*. Grand Rapids: Eerdmans, 1989.
Downey, Glanville. *Constantinople in the Age of Justinian*. The Centers of Civilization. Norman: University of Oklahoma Press, 1960.
Gossip, Arthur John. "The Gospel according to St. John, Exposition." In *The Interpreter's Bible*, edited by George Arthur Buttrick, 8:437–811. 12 vols. Nashville: Abingdon, 1980.
Heschel, Abraham J. *The Prophets Part II*. New York: Harper Torchbooks, 1962.
Long, Thomas G. *Hebrews*. Interpretation: A Bible Commentary for Teaching and Preaching. Louisville: John Knox, 1997.
MacLeod, Alistair. *No Great Mischief*. Toronto: McClelland and Stewart, 1999.
McNeill, John T., ed. *Calvin: Institutes of the Christian Religion: Books III.XX to IV.XX*. Translated by Ford Lewis Battles. Library of Christian Classics 21. Philadelphia: Westminster, 1960.
National Park Service. "Lincoln's Second Inaugural Address." https://www.nps.gov/linc/learn/historyculture/lincoln-second-inaugural.htm.
The Office of Worship for the Presbyterian Church (U.S.A.) and the Cumberland Presbyterian Church. *The Funeral: A Service of Witness to the Resurrection*. The Worship of God, Supplemental Liturgical Resource 4. Philadelphia: Westminster, 1986.
Saliers, Don E. *Worship Come to Its Senses*. Nashville: Abingdon, 1996.

www.ingramcontent.com/pod-product-compliance
Lightning Source LLC
Chambersburg PA
CBHW071451150426
43191CB00008B/1304